# Willingly ACT for Spiritual Development: Acknowledge, Choose, & Teach Others

## Hank Robb, Ph.D., ABPP

Valued Living Books, Inc.
10 Monroe Blvd.
Suite 6S
Long Beach, NY 11561
www.valuedlivingbooks.com

# Publisher's Note

This publication is designed to provide accurate and authoritative information regarding the subject matter covered. It is sold with the understanding that the publisher is not engaged in rendering psychological services. If expert assistance or counseling is needed, the services of a professional should be sought.

# Table of Contents

# Foreword

Spiritual development blesses us at unanticipated moments. Several of my personal blessings came during science conferences. Other blessings alighted at an ice cream parlor, a walk in an urban park, and while drinking a pint in a Dublin pub. Each of these particular instances arose while speaking with my dear friend, Hank Robb.

Hank and I have spent time together in many different parts of the world, and it is always a pleasure to learn from him. Our conversation themes vary, but we typically end up casually quipping about the meaning of life or some other amusing topic. Hank's affable and humorous way of bestowing his wealth of wisdom has helped plenty of people over the years. He's a skillful therapist, educator, and applied scientist. Even though Hank and I have studied much of the same subjects, he seems to reliably provide unique perspectives on topics that act as linchpins for deeper insights.

*Willingly ACT for Spiritual Development* provides these guiding perspectives, linchpins, and insights. Dr. Robb has the education, experience, and acumen to guide you on a journey of intentional living for yourself and for the ones you love.

This book is Hank's voice speaking to you… genuinely and unvarnished. I hope you read his words as if he were talking to you at a behavioral science conference, or an ice cream parlor… or a Dublin pub. And I hope his words are a blessing to you.

◎ D.J. Moran, Ph.D., BCBA-D

# Acknowledgements

There are many individuals behind the words of this book. Some I studied and trained with. Others I only read or listened to. By providing the list below, I hope to both give credit and appreciation for my opportunities with these individuals and their work as well as to provide the potential reader with some sense of the intellectual background for this book.

As a college student, Professor Gale Fuller introduced me to the world of Humanistic Psychology, especially Carl Rogers and Abraham Maslow, and suggested the possibility of finding something in life you would do for nothing and then getting someone to pay you to do it. In graduate school, Professor Lyle Eddy tutored me though the work of American Pragmatists, particularly the work of John Dewey. I also studied Radical Behaviorism, particularly the work of B. F. Skinner as well as the Structuralism and Genetic Epistemology of Jean Piaget. Following graduate school, I trained in what is now called Rational Emotive Behavior Therapy with Albert Ellis and have been additionally influenced by his training colleagues Richard Wessler and Ray DiGiuseppe. I became greatly influenced by the work of the American mythologist Joseph Campbell. Most recently, I am influenced by Steven Hayes, Kirk Strosahl, Kelly Wilson, Dermot Barnes-Holmes, Yvonne Barnes-Holmes, Carmen Luciano, and my additional colleagues from the world of Acceptance & Commitment Therapy and Relational Frame Theory.

# Preface

I wrote this book because there are many individuals who consider themselves to be spiritual but not religious. There are also individuals who are religious but do not find their religion nurtures their spiritual dimension. On my way to becoming licensed to practice psychology, I learned quite a bit about the sensations and actions associated with the human body and the thoughts and images associated with the human mind. However, I have not found that the mind's thoughts and images or the body's sensations and actions are enough to understand the psychological dimension of human beings. That more complete understanding requires consideration of an additional dimension: the spiritual dimension.

Historically, this spiritual dimension has been missing for folks who train in science because of what we might call the assumption of two worlds, one natural and the other supernatural. While the body and mind are assigned to the natural world, the spiritual dimension of humanity is assigned to the supernatural world and, thus, off limits to those studying the natural one. This is the reason my academic training was limited to body and mind.

But suppose there is one whole universe that we are not only a part of, but also able to explore and put to our use. In that case, the spiritual aspect of humanity is no longer off limits to psychological examination. This book is the result of my life experience pushing me in that direction. It demonstrates one way, though I am sure not the only way, of identifying, cultivating, and applying each human being's spiritual dimension for the purpose of living a more deeply fulfilling human life right here, right now. It is not about some other time or some other place. It is not about some form of being other than the very human form that is reading these words.

The A-C-T in *Willingly ACT for Spiritual Development* stands for Acknowledge, Choose, and Teach others. First, willingly acknowledge the world as it is, was, or may be. Second, willingly choose and willingly serve the "Leading Principles" that identify your life directions and the "values" that identify the manner you want to travel no matter in which direction you are going and that together make up Big Picture of your life. Finally, willingly teach others to do the same. You are encouraged to ACT willingly because ACT-ing grudgingly only makes ACT-ing harder to do.

My hope is that reading this book, and acting on what you read, will provide you with a more deeply fulfilling human life right here, right now. Unfortunately, there will never be enough people who will read this book and implement its principles to make a difference for humanity and for humanity's home, this beautiful blue marble spinning in the blackness of space. But if enough people teach others the principles in this book, there just might be. That is why Teaching completes the acronym "ACT." Knowing what to do can be important. However, knowing what to do isn't doing it. The fruit of reading this book will be found in moving your hands, arms, feet, and mouth so as to willingly acknowledge, willing choose, and willingly teach others.

# Chapter 1
## The Context

We humans desire. We want. That's how we are.

Wants or desires are not needs. The word "need" simply shows a connection between what we want and a means to fulfill that want. If I want cooked food, I need both food and a means to cook it. I only *need* the means to stay alive, such as food, air, and water, if I *want* to stay alive in the first place.

A second fundamental thing about we humans is that we live in a world where we don't always get what we want, and often do get what we don't want. Thus, living as a human being means experiencing sorrow, the natural response to not getting what we want as well as getting what we don't. The amount of sorrow largely depends on the depth of our desires. Not much desire – not much sorrow. Great desire – great sorrow. At the shallow end of the pool of sorrow is feeling sad or disappointed. With more sorrow, tears come out of our eyes. With more, cries come out of our throat. With more, mucus comes out of our nose. With enough sorrow, our entire body shakes. The deep end of the pool feels like it has no bottom even as we strain with our toes to touch that bottom and bounce ourselves back to the surface. Yet, without sensing that we have touched bottom, we eventually experience our head having popped back above the waters of sorrow. And then, we either have another dunk, move to the shallow end of the pool and step out, or find the waters of sorrow have simply evaporated.

Since humans desire in a world where desires frequently go unfulfilled, which makes sorrow inevitable, you might think the ability to effectively address sorrow would be a well-cultivated skill for all humanity. Almost the opposite is true. Said bluntly, sorrow is like poop. It will pass through us if we let it.

Lie down, fully engulfed by the tears, sobs, mucus and shaking of sorrow and, in a while, you will notice it has stopped, or you fall asleep and wake up and notice that it's stopped. And then? You get up and do the next thing! As hard as it sometimes is to believe, life actually goes on.

Instead of learning to willingly let sorrow pass through us, we quite often try to hide sorrow from ourselves and from others or deaden it with some form of anesthesia. This training often starts early. Tearful children may be comforted but often enough they are scolded, called names like "cry baby" or simply told to "stop it" or "shut up." "Stop that crying or I'll give you something to cry about" lives in the life history of many.

Far too often, we are not comforted while patiently and thoroughly taught to willingly let the tears, cries, mucus, and bodily shaking of sorrow pass through us. Nor are we thought to do the same for others. Instead, we are mostly left on our own to figure out how to hide or avoid our own sorrow and to turn away from the sorrow of others even as we pretend not to have noticed it in the first place. Rather than responding with the comforting closeness that can help ease or better carry our pain, letting others know that the world has wounded our heart often leads to even more pain when we are told we are "being weak," "breaking down" or "acting like a child."

Soon we no longer require anyone else to belittle us in these ways because we have taken up the chants ourselves. Only at the funerals of our dearest loved ones may we be permitted a tear or two. Even then we are constantly on guard lest we break down, as though sorrow were evidence of a machine that malfunctioned rather than a human being experiencing the pain of desires going unfulfilled.

Like those who fail to realize that courage is not the absence of fear but making something more important than being afraid, we buy the frequently offered nonsense that emotional strength is being so hardened to life that our heart can no longer be touched by it. Better for us to recognize that emotional strength is fully and willingly embracing the pain that comes from caring and continuing to care anyway. The pain of sorrow is simply the price that comes with truly giving a rip rather than remaining breezily indifferent or emotionally deadened. The "honk, honk, honk" as you clear your nose and mop up your tears are as natural to being overwhelmed by sorrow as loud and uncontrolled cackling is to being overwhelmed by laughter. But who has ever been told their uncontrolled laughter is evidence of emotional break down?

Many have become so well practiced at blunting sorrow that, when actively attempting to resist their long-practiced resistance to experiencing sorrow, they experience letting sorrow come as making themselves feel sad. That making-myself-feel-sad experience is the result of attempting to resist, in the current moment, the long practiced and well-established habit of resisting contact with sorrow. From the inside out, resisting that resistance produces the sense that one is making oneself sad rather than allowing the experience of what is already there – namely sorrow. Those who compulsively throw themselves into activities like work, sex, exercise or eating demonstrate additional ways to avoid contacting sorrow.

Attempting to distract ourselves from sorrow creates one set of difficulties but life really goes sideways once we start escaping sorrow through various forms of anesthesia. Alcohol and other substances are common but so is righteous indignation.

Many find that psychological place individuals can go and feel nothing at all. The upside is you don't feel the pain of sorrow. The downside is not feeling anything. Growing tired of feeling nothing at all, people leave that spot, experience their sorrow, and soon return to that place of feeling nothing at all. As with other attempts to avoid or anesthetize sorrow, the vicious cycle just goes round and round.

Some have suggested the best response to these facts is to just stop wanting anything. No desire equals no sorrow! One trouble with this approach is that it requires us to stop wanting to stop wanting. That isn't the approach offered here.

## Fulfillment

Sometimes we do get what we want, and the name sued here for that experience is "fulfillment." Some fulfillments are rather like the spun sugar confection that people where I'm from call "cotton candy." Cotton candy tastes good in the moment but it won't sustain you. Other fulfillments are more like vegetables. Regardless of how they taste in the moment, they do sustain you. Other people, and society in general, can offer advice about which fulfillments are more like cotton candy and which are more like vegetables, and which are somewhere in between. If we are patient and careful, our own experience will teach us which fulfillments sustain us, and which do not. And our own experience is often our best teacher. Thus, life as a human being is sorrow, and more or less, sustaining fulfillments.

## Our Relationship to Life

We also have a relationship to our life as a human being. We can willingly acknowledge, grudgingly acknowledge, or refuse to acknowledge human life as filled with sorrow along with more, or less, sustaining fulfilments. In English the word "accept" often comes across as something rather passive. That is, in part, why I chose the phrase "willingly acknowledge," though "accept" can be understood to mean the same thing. Another way we can indicate the relationship I am pointing to is to say we can give, rather than withhold, our permission for life to be as it is, namely, sorrow and fulfillments.

Willingly acknowledging is not the same as approving. I would be more likely to approve of life if I always quickly and easily got what I want and if my fulfillments were always deeply sustaining. One might say that humans don't seem to have been on the committee when it came to the creation of life! Even so, here we are. Life is as it is: sorrow and more, or less, sustaining fulfillments. How do we relate to these facts? Do we willing acknowledge, do we accept, or give our permission for life to be as it is, or are we grudging, non-accepting, permission withholding or refusing to acknowledge life as we actually find it? We don't get to choose how life is. We do get to choose how we relate to it. We can willingly acknowledge the world as it is, was or may be. It's an option, a possibility, a choice.

In the approach I am advocating here, I will use the word *"happiness,"* to mean willingly acknowledging, accepting, or giving your permission for life to be as it is, and *"unhappiness"* to mean being grudging, unaccepting or withholding your permission.

The rest of this book is not about pitting fulfillments against happiness and asking us to side with one or the other. It is about pursuing both at the same time. The rest of this book is not about pitting fulfillments against sorrow. It is about making peace with sorrow as an inevitable part of life as we pursue our deepest and most sustaining fulfillments.

4

# Chapter 2
## Mind, Body, Spirit & More

Most of us readily recognize that we have a body. And, in some important sense, we *are* our body. If we are lucky, we have hands, arms, feet, and a mouth. If we are lucky, our body allows us to see, hear, touch, smell, taste, and move about.

Most of us also recognize that we have a mind. We experience thoughts, images, and bodily sensations. Mentally, we hear things no one is saying. Mentally, I can think, "I am sitting in a chair." No one else is saying those words and I am not saying them out loud. Yet, I can readily hear them. Mentally, we have images when the thing isn't there. I can see a flag flying at a sports stadium even as I am sitting in a windowless room, and I can see my mother's face though she died many years ago. If one of my daughters were to say, "You have ruined my life and I never want to see you again," and I took those words seriously, I would feel great pain though she had never laid a hand on me. This is an odd thing. We do not seem to hear our thoughts with our ears or see our images with our eyes, but we do seem to feel this mental pain with our bodies. Because we can feel without being touched, I grouped bodily sensations with thoughts and images.

While most of us readily recognize that we have a body and a mind, we often are not so familiar with our spirit. When that word is used, most people imagine something otherworldly. And yet, our spirit is as common as our hands, arms, feet, and mouth or thoughts, images, and bodily sensations. Here is a way that usually allows individuals to make contact with the spiritual aspect of their being.

### Activity 1: The Place-From-Which

*Notice anything – including the words you are reading. I am not asking you to take the mental action of having thoughts such as, "I am noticing." I'm asking that you to take a different action: the action of noticing. And if, while you are noticing, I ask you, "Who's doing that?" you will very likely think or say, "me," or "I am." Now it should be quite clear that the noticing is not words such as "me," or "I am" or any form of speech. Those words are pointing to an aspect of your being from which you are doing the noticing and that* *aspect is not anything mental in the sense that it is not more thoughts, images, or bodily sensations. Rather, it is a place-from-which. It is a place from which you can <u>notice</u> thoughts, images, bodily sensations as well as the world outside your skin. Interestingly, it is a place from which you can even notice that you are noticing and even notice that you are noticing, noticing. For example, I can notice you, noticing me as I notice you! This place is different from your mind producing thoughts such as, "I am noticing that I am noticing," but a place from which you can actually take the action of noticing that you are noticing or noticing that you are noticing that you are noticing. Take a moment and see if in addition to noticing, you can also notice <u>that</u> you are noticing or even notice that what you are noticing is noticing.*

I suggest that place-from-which is the third aspect of the little triplet: mind, body, spirit. Or, said a little differently, that place-from-which is the spiritual aspect of your being.

This spiritual you has been there a long time. Think back to when you were a young child. You had a rather different body than the one you have now. You had a rather different mind than the one you have now. And yet, this aspect of you that notices, and notices noticing, was not only there then, but, importantly, it was there, then, pretty much the same way it is here, now. Over the years you have known joy, sorrow, anger, fear, and any number of other emotions. Some, and perhaps all, of these may have been very strong in some moments, and in the moment experienced, very powerful. And yet your noticing ability has not been changed by having noticed any of them regardless of how intense or powerful they may have been at the time they were noticed. Even as your body and mind have changed quite a bit from those childhood days, this spiritual aspect of your being has changed very little, if at all. Additionally, you most likely cannot recall a time when this, relatively unchanging, spiritual aspect of you wasn't there.

So, from our spiritual aspect, we: 1) notice, 2) notice we are noticing, as well as 3) notice that we are noticing our own noticing or the noticing of another (I notice you, noticing me, noticing you). Fourthly, this spiritual aspect of our existence has been around, pretty much unchanged, for about as long as we can remember.

Many find that their spirit has a fifth aspect that is similar to the eye of a hurricane. Around the outside of a hurricane winds are blowing, often quite powerfully. At the eye of the hurricane there is a calm stability even as winds blow powerfully around that stable center. Many can make contact with the calm stability of their spiritual center even as thoughts, images, and bodily sensations whirl around that center, sometimes with great force.

Everyone has been very frightened at one time or another. Many also will be able to recall a time when they were both very frightened and, at the same time, had a sense of calm stability. We might say that in such moments we are not only in contact with our thoughts, images, bodily sensations, and the world around us, but also with the spiritual aspect of our being. Since humans are often looking for something that is stable in life, it is useful to be able make contact with the spiritual aspect of our being – by analogy, the eye at the center of the hurricane of living.

There is a sixth quality that many can notice about this spiritual aspect of themselves. If you contact your own spirit, you may notice a sort of aliveness, with no real sense of goodness or badness. It is the same when we spiritually contact the world around us. The buzz here, within us, is there – in the tree, in our pet, in our parent, in our child. We spiritually connect with the world around us as simply buzz. Interestingly, some find it easier to contact this buzz of being outside, rather than inside, their skin. And so, people search for expansive vistas, thundering waterfalls, or gaze into the eyes of their pets in an effort to contact this experience.

From your spiritual center, your mind and body can be experienced as things that you have rather than things that you are. From your spiritual center a phrase like, "I have a mind and I have a body" in the same way I might have a coat or shoes actually seems to fit your experience. A strong mind and strong body are possessions more valuable than a weak mind and body. And yet, regardless of the value of your possessions, from your spiritual center, they remain exactly that – things you possess.

There is a seventh important aspect about our spiritual center – a sense of bodily control. We can think, "I will not raise my right hand," and we can raise it. We can think, "I will raise my left hand," and not raise it. We can feel very fearful of going toward something and go toward it. We can have a very strong urge to go toward something and not do so. When we are acting from our spiritual center, then regardless of what inducements the world offers us to act in one way, or how much our body and mind push us to act that way, we have no doubt that we can still act otherwise. Conversely, when we act from the spiritual aspect of our being, then, no matter what threats the world makes toward us if we act, or do not act, in a certain way or how much our body and mind push us to avoid doing so, we have no doubt that we can still do otherwise. We might say that, when operating from our spirit, our body does whatever we pick to be done regardless of the circumstances inside or outside our skin. Perhaps we speak with a stammer, and yet we still speak. Perhaps we walk toward, or away, reluctantly, and yet we still walk. Perhaps our body shakes with the desire to strike out, and yet we do not strike.

### Activity 2: I Cannot Walk

*Seat yourself in a room at a little distance from the entrance to the room. If the room you are using has more than one entrance, then pick one for the purpose of this activity. Cup your hands. Imagine you are holding a feather in you cupped hands. It is gentle, and you can hold it gently. Now imagine you are holding a cactus fruit with many painful spines. The cactus is not gentle, yet you can hold it gently. You sense that what you hold does not determine the manner or way you hold it and that whatever you hold can be held gently. While you imagine holding the painful spikey cactus, begin saying, out loud, and over and over, "I cannot walk over to the entrance and back with this much pain." Then, while you are saying, "I cannot walk over to the entrance and back with this much pain," walk over to the entrance and back. Once you are again seated, switch to repeating this phrase, "I cannot stay seated with this much pain, I must stand up." Say it several times even as you remain seated.*

The point of this activity is to explode the common illusion that we will surely lose control of our hands, arms, feet, and mouth when we have the "wrong" thoughts, images and bodily sensations and the only way to get that control back is to somehow get the "right" thoughts, images, and bodily sensations back into us. It often does seem this way when we function as if we can only act from our mind and body. Yet, if we act from the spiritual aspect of our being, it doesn't, necessarily, work this way. From our spiritual center, we can hear ourselves thinking, "No one wants to hear from me," and speak anyway. We can feel like calling someone a nasty name and refrain from saying it. We can feel afraid to reach out to someone, and still reach out. We can hear someone's comments and have the thought, "Those are the words of a complete fool," and kindly say, "I have a different view." As John Lennon and Paul McCartney of The Beatles are credited with so aptly pointing out, when it comes to acting from the spiritual aspect of your being, "There's nothing you can do that can't be done" and it doesn't, necessarily require "getting your feelings right," or "your mind straight" first.

This illusion joins a number of others. One of my favorites is sunrise and sunset. If you get up while it is still dark and the sky has few clouds, go outside, face East with your eyes open and wait long enough, it will certainly seem that the sun rises. Anyone in a situation like the one I have described who does not find that the sun seems to be rising is either blind or on some serious drugs! Then, wait a few hours. If the sky stays clear, you are outside, and wait long enough while facing West with your eyes open, it will certainly seem that the sun sets. Newspapers, and even the Internet, still provide the time of sunrise and sunset rather than earth turn. However, the sun does not rise or set even though it seems to and even though many people on our planet are still persuaded by the illusion. The earth turns. The rising and setting of the sun is a powerful illusion. And, an illusion nonetheless!

It is the same with the control of our hands, arms, feet, mouth, and the rest of our body parts. When acting from our spiritual center, we do not need to get all the wrong thoughts, images, and bodily sensations out of us and get all the right ones into us in order to exert control over our body. From the spiritual aspect of our being, we have direct control of our body generally and, of particular importance, control of our hands, arms, feet, and mouth. We don't have to first get rid of feelings of fear or thoughts like, "It will be awful if they reject me and my ideas" or replace them with different feelings and thoughts in order to speak. And, when acting from our spiritual center, we are certain we can speak even while having those feelings and thoughts, and even if we stammer and stutter while doing so.

The certainty of control we sense for our body when acting from our spiritual center does not extend to our thoughts, images, and bodily sensations. We cannot always pick these the way we can pick what we do with our hands, arms, feet, and mouth. I grew up learning certain childhood rhymes. One went, "Jack and Jill went up the ...".

If you are a native English speaker with a history similar to mine, there is a very good chance you heard "hill" when you read the words above even though that last word of the rhyme wasn't printed on the page. You might exert excellent control over not saying "hill," and yet still find yourself thinking it. Many have had a similar experience when trying to think something different.

"OK, instead of thinking 'hill,' I'll think 'mountain.'"

Sure enough, the first few times you think mountain. However, it isn't very long before you think, "Wow, this is really working! I'm not thinking ....". And, there "hill" is again. Thus, you may vow that you will never again think, "What a loser I am!" when you make a mistake. "I will instead only think, 'People make mistakes.'" It may even work for a while. But, soon enough, you make a mistake and there it is again, "What a loser I am!"

When acting from our spiritual center, rather than from our mind or body, we have good control of our bodily actions regardless of our thoughts, images and sensations and we have no doubt about that control. When it comes to having the same kind of control of our thoughts, images, and sensations - not so much!

If we require that we "feel confident" before we speak up, we may never speak up at all because picking what we think and feel is a lot less controllable than picking what we do with our hands, arms, feet, and mouth, even when operating from our spiritual center. And yet, as long as we act from our spiritual center, then picking what we do with our hands, arms, feet, and mouth remains in our control, even when our thoughts and feelings insist that it does not. When acting from our spiritual center, then even if we are mentally stewing, we can still be bodily doing.

This picking what we do brings us to another aspect of our spirit. It is another kind of picking. While we may not be able to pick if we act anxiously or un-anxiously, there are certain ways of acting that we can pick when that picking is done from our spiritual center. One of the most important of these ways of acting is picking willingly, rather than grudgingly, as the way, or manner, we do whatever we do. Just as there is nothing we can do that can't be done, there is nothing we can do that can't be done willingly. Since doing things grudgingly is inevitably more energy sapping than doing things willingly, our ability to pick willingly as the way we do anything we pick to do is, indeed, an especially fortunate aspect of our place-from-which. It is from our spiritual center that we can bring happiness to our world of sorrow by living in it willingly rather than grudgingly.

Our spiritual center allows one additional type of picking. Just as we can pick what we do with our hands, arms, feet, and mouth and pick to do it willingly, we also can pick what we make important with those actions. When acting spiritually, we can make important whatever we choose to make important, regardless of the circumstances around us or our thoughts, images, or bodily sensations.

Whether we act, or remain still, something is being made important. As long as we are breathing, we are making something important, if only to continue breathing. Because we humans can move our bodies as well as feel, think, image, notice, and at the same time notice that we are noticing, we can discern what is being made important and then continue picking that or pick something else. Additionally, because we humans can move our bodies as well as feel, think, image, notice, and at the same time notice that we are noticing, we can discern what we might make important, and pick that.

## Who Am I *Really*?

The advantage of relating to our mind and our body as things that we have rather than things that we are is that we no longer required to do what our mind says or our body urges. Unfortunately, our spiritual dimension does not allow us, at any moment we choose, to think, imagine, or feel whatever we would like to think, imagine, or feel, nor avoid thinking, imagining, or feeling whatever we would like not to. However, our spiritual dimension is the place from which we can willingly acknowledge these thoughts, images and bodily sensations while also willingly choosing what we do with our hands, arms, feet, and mouth regardless of what we are thinking, imagining, or feeling. The spiritual aspect of our being opens the possibility of willingly choosing what we make important in our life and then willingly acting in the service of what we have chosen. This is the advantage of being able to relate to our mind and body as things we have rather than things we are.

However, this advantage also comes with a difficulty. From the possession perspective of "I have a mind and a body," it is easy to either begin wondering, "Who am I really?" or to conclude, "My spiritual dimension is the real me." Thus, I suggest adding the phrase, "and more," when chasing, or being chased by, the question, "Who am I really?" I am my body and more. I am my mind and more. I am my spirit and more.

Your hand is neither your foot nor your nose. And your hand, foot and nose are all your body. Similarly, your body is neither your mind, nor your spirit, and all are you. And you are even more. Not only are you your mind, body, and spirit but you are also all you have done up to this moment – and you are even more than that.

In addition to your mind, body, spirit, and all you have done up to now, you are also, in every moment, all you might do. Because there is nothing you can do that can't be done, all that possibility is also you. In every moment, including right here, right now, there is the possibility of doing anything that you can, in fact, do. That includes the possibility of acting out of habit or exerting your power to willingly choose, a power provided by your spiritual dimension. And all of that is also you!

The aim of the approach suggested here is not for anyone to ultimately identify themselves with only one aspect of their being in contrast to other aspects just as it is not the aim of this approach to encourage the pursuit of fulfillment over happiness or happiness over fulfillment. Rather, this approach encourages recognizing all aspects of your being as exactly that – all you – body, mind, spirit, all that I have done and all that I might do. Only by including all five can you fully answer the question, "Who am I really?" even as it will also sometimes be useful, from your spiritual dimension, to regard your mind and body with their insistent thoughts, images and urges as things I possess rather than things I am.

To summarize, the spiritual aspect of our being includes:(1) noticing, (2) noticing that we are noticing, (3) noticing that we are noticing our own noticing or the noticing of another, (4) a sense of having been there for about as long as we can remember without being changed by what has been noticed, (5) a sense of stability, like the eye of a hurricane, (6) the "buzz of being" rather than an evaluation, (7) the sense of having or possessing a mind and a body rather than being one or both of them, (8) sensing a certainty of bodily control without regard to thoughts, images or bodily sensations, (9) the ability to pick what we do with our body, (10) the ability take actions willingly rather than grudgingly, and (11) the ability to pick what we put our actions in the service of.

*This brings us to the aim of this book, namely, spiritual development - developing our ability to willingly pick what we make important within the context of our life as a human being: a life of sorrows and fulfillments and the choice to willingly acknowledge the very nature of our existence; developing the skill to willingly act from the eye of the hurricane and maintain contact with the buzz of being.*

# Chapter 3
## The Formula for Human Liberation

*By willingly doing something unpleasant, and willingly refusing to do something pleasant, in the service of something I willingly choose to make more important, I never have to be a slave to circumstance.*

These few words describe how to live life spiritually. They describe what it takes to live life no longer under the control of the moment. No longer being controlled by whatever thoughts or feelings that happen to show up. No longer being controlled by whatever is going on in the world around us at any given time.

We all had a chance to learn this formula when we were children, especially going to school. Many of us missed it. I know I did! If we go to school long enough, we will be given homework. And, more importantly, it will be homework that we don't want to do. However, in the service of things like actually learning something, or simply making better grades, we can do the unpleasant homework and not do things that would be a lot more pleasant. And, we could also have learned to do these things willingly rather than grudgingly. In my case, if homework did get done, it rarely got done willingly!

Willingly doing homework that we don't want to do is an early instance of spiritual development because we are learning that we do not have to be controlled by immediate circumstance. We can transcend the moment and make something more important than our immediate surroundings or our immediate thoughts or our immediate feelings. In those moments, our body isn't running the show, nor are our thoughts, images, or the world around us. The spiritual aspect of our being, the part from which we notice and pick, is growing stronger by being put to use. Like many other things in life, the more we practice, the better we get. How far can we go spiritually? The answer flows from how persistently we practice. Formulating and following our Leading Principles is one important thing to practice.

## Leading Principles

Something more must be said about "in the service of something I make more important." If you hold a compass, it will point to magnetic North. And, if you started moving in that direction, and you were continually provided with enough support, you could eventually reach that place on the earth we call magnetic North. When you got there, the compass needle would no longer have a particular direction in which to point and every time you walked away, it would point you right back to the place you just left.

However, if you took that same compass, and went either East or West, you would never come to a place like magnetic North. You would be able to keep going and going and going. No matter how far East you went, there would still be more East. No matter how far West you went, there would still be more West. What I call "Leading Principles" work like that. No matter how far you go, they will lead you further.

Leading Principles are not goals. Goals are places at which you can actually arrive. If you are able to attend secondary school, and you set the goal of graduating, then, if you work hard, you very likely will achieve that goal – you graduate.

But suppose you pick, "Be the best educated person I can be." When would you finish that? No matter how well educated you became, you could get up the next day and still be led by that principle – "Be the best educated person I can be." You can just keep going, and going, and going.

Consider marriage. Well, there's probably somebody! OK, so now you are married – goal achieved. But suppose you pick "Be the best mate I can be." When would you finish that? No matter how good a mate you have been, you could get up the next day and still be led by, "Be the best mate I can be" – and the next day, and the next. There, literally, could be no end to it. In fact, if you had been a lousy mate for some time, you could still get up the next day and pick, "Be the best mate I can be," as a Leading Principle, and follow it. You wouldn't have to feel like it" You could just do it – willingly! You would not be starting from the same place as you would be if you had been following that Leading Principle for several years, and you could still start. If you divorced, you could even pick, "Be the best ex-mate I can be!"

Consider having a child. You could adopt or have one the usual way. Once again – goal achieved. You now have a child. But suppose you pick, "Be the best parent I can be." When would you finish that? What children need at two is not what they need at thirty-two and a good parent knows the difference! No matter how old your child gets, you can still pick, and follow, "Be the best parent I can be."

Leading Principles are directions in life just as East and West are directions. They are not goals. They are not places at which you arrive while moving in a certain direction. Rather, they are particular directions in which a person can choose to move. However, no one can move in more than one direction at the same time and almost all of us will choose more than one Leading Principle for our lives.

Living life as a one-pointed meditation is easy enough, this - and nothing else. People who are sometimes called "workaholics" live this way, work – and nothing else. Living with more than one Leading Principle raises the issue of balance, a life that includes not only a Leading Principle such as "be the best educated person I can be", but also "be the best mate I can be," as well as "be the best parent I can be." If you have ever tried literally balancing on something like a balance ball or other balance-practice device, or even balancing on a bicycle, you will notice that you are rarely in a state of exact balance. Instead, you are, typically, a little out of balance in one direction, make a correction and then find yourself a little out of balance in a different direction. In truth, living a balanced life will most often be experienced as feeling you are, somewhat out of balance and in need of correction and you will rarely, if ever, have the sense of living your life in perfect balance. Nothing's wrong! That's simply how living a balanced life works.

Looking at things from a spiritual point of view, there are some interesting things we can notice about any Leading Principle. We can follow it right now, in this very moment, and no matter how many moments we follow it, the Leading Principle is never used up – it can go on and on and on. If we want to make these points using language sometimes used when speaking about spiritual things, we can say this about any Leading Principle. When followed, it is both imminent, it is right here, and infinite, it is never used up.

Additionally, by following a Leading Principle in the moment in which we are actually in, we are no longer controlled by other circumstances of that moment such as our thoughts or feelings or what others around us are doing, including what they are telling us to do. Thus, again said in a fancy way, it is both imminent, it is right now, and transcendent, it is beyond right now. As long as we are alive, developing the spiritual aspect of our being means developing our ability to, in this very moment, forever and always, transcend what we experience in this very moment should we choose to do so.

**Values**

In addition to going in a direction, there is the manner or way you travel in that direction. I might walk West. I might also run, crawl, drive, fly, or swim West. I will use the word "value" to indicate the manner or way you choose to travel without much regard to which direction you are traveling. As we have already seen, one way to travel is willingly as compared to grudgingly or some other form of unwillingness. Consider traveling kindly. You could go West kindly or you could go East kindly. Consider traveling meanly. You could go West meanly, or you could go East meanly. Just as you develop your ability to pick the principles that lead you, you can also develop your ability to pick the manner or way you follow. You can develop your ability to pick what you value, no matter the direction in which you travel. It is hard to imagine being a good mate and not picking kindly as a way of acting. Yet, if you never chose a person with whom to build your life, you could still pick kindly as a way to do your work even as you also could pick doing your work unkindly. From the spiritual aspect of your being, it's a choice. From the perspective presented here, Leading Principles tell the directions we are choosing while values tell the manner we move in those directions. Both are important.

Some may have seen a television, or other type of screen, with a picture-in-a-picture feature. There is one thing shown in a little picture in one corner of the screen and something else shown in the much bigger picture filling the rest of the screen. By analogy, we all can be said to be living in the little picture of our life – the moment we are actually in. However, we don't have to live for the little picture only. We could live for the Big Picture of the life we are choosing to life.

Focusing on our Big Picture, which is made up of our Leading Principles and values, allows us to live in the little picture of this moment; indeed, where else can we literally be but right here right now, while not living only for the little picture of this moment. We do this by using words and images to construct the Big Picture we want for our life, a picture that illustrates the directions we want to travel in our lives and the manner in which we want to travel no matter the direction we go, and then acting in the service of that Big Picture. To be clear, I am not talking about avoiding the experience of the moment. I am talking about having the experience of the moment and more. I am talking about transcending the moment by putting your "eyes on the prize" of the Big Picture you created for your life.

Spiritual development, in and of itself, is not about which Leading Principles and values you pick. It is about the very act of you picking the Leading Principles you follow and the manner in which you follow them rather than handing the choice over to someone, or something, else. You could pick, "Be the worst educated person I can be" or, "Be the most average mate I can be." If you made such choices, you would still be noticing, noticing that you are noticing and picking. You would not be living life like a leaf blown here and there by the wind, responding only to the circumstances of the moment. You would be putting your actions in the service of something beyond merely the moment you are literally in. You could still be doing something unpleasant and refusing to do something pleasant in the service of something you make more important such as, "Grudgingly being as mediocre a parent as I can be." Following that value and Leading Principle might not be the kind of spiritual development that interests you. I know it doesn't interest me. However, the point is that it would be a kind of spiritual development because spiritual development is about you being the author of your own life, or said slightly differently, spiritual development is about you choosing what you make important in your life.

Spiritual development is waking up to the fact that your feelings don't have to run your life, and neither do your thoughts or images, or the people around you, or your life circumstances. *Spiritual development is waking up to the spiritual aspect of your being. It is about waking up to that place from which you can pick your Leading Principles and values and from which you then exercise your ability to put your actions in the service of the Leading Principles and values you pick regardless of any other factors such as thoughts, images, feelings, other people, or life circumstances.*

Spiritual development is not about the choices you make, it is about you making choices. Spiritual development involves picking and following both Leading Principles and values but, in and of itself, developing spiritually doesn't say what those Leading Principles and values must be. Spiritual development is about developing your ability to be up to something, but the something is up to you. You could pick, "Willingly be the best student I can be." But you could also pick, "Grudgingly be the worst student I can be." If you picked "Grudgingly be the worst student I can be" things would not be easy. It can be very hard on a person to grudgingly refuse to learn no matter what. It might be doable, but you would definitely have to do things that were unpleasant and refuse to do things that were pleasant in the service of that Leading Principle.

### Activity 3: The Palm Technique

*This activity is designed to clarify what activities are consistent with a Leading Principle or value and which are not. It begins by selecting a symbol for a Leading Principle or value. When I suggest, "symbol," I am reminded of a Medieval European crest. These devices consist of pictures and words, in the case of European crests the words are usually in Latin. They are not the family itself but symbolize the family. So, begin with something that symbolizes the Leading Principle or value under consideration. For example, a very simple symbol for the Leading Principle: Be the best mate I can be, might be a heart shape with a picture of one's mate inside the heart. A very simple symbol for the value of acting compassionately, might simply be a heart all by itself. You can make the symbol as simple or as complex as you like. The important point is that whatever symbol you create, it should, for you, capture the essence of the Leading Principle or value.*

*Next, fully extend one of your arms with the palm of your hand turned up, or said slightly differently, with the palm of your hand facing you. Now, as much as you can, project your symbol on to your upturned palm. If fully successful, you will literally see the symbol on the palm of your hand. Alternatively, you may only sense it.*

*With the symbol on the upturned palm of your fully extended arm, look down your arm to see what behaviors, literally, line up with the symbol you have chosen. If you look to either side of your arm, there will also be any number of behaviors that you could do but which do not line up or fit with the symbolic representation of Leading Principle or value under consideration.*

*If you focus on doing the behaviors on your arm, the behaviors that fit with or line up with your symbol, the ones off your arm will, in an important sense, take care of themselves. You won't have to concern yourself with not doing them because you will already be doing something else, namely one, or more, of the behaviors on your arm that line up with or fit with the symbol on you palm.*

*Though, spiritually speaking, one does not have to feel like performing an action, to do it, the Palm Technique can help provide some level of motivation, or "feeling like it." Look on your arm and find a behavior that lines up with the symbol on your palm but is not a particularly appealing activity to you at this moment. Once you have found such an action, take a few moments to focus on the relationship between that behavior and the symbol on your palm. Looking at the behavior all by itself is one thing. Seeing the connection, between that behavior and the Leading Principle or value that you have chosen for the Big Picture of your life can be quite another. When individuals recognize such behaviors, even unpleasant ones, as the means for bringing one of their very own Leading Principles or values into actual concrete existence in the world in which they are currently living, those individuals often report being more energized, or motivated, to take those actions. Try it for yourself and see.*

# Chapter 4
## The Formula for Serenity in Action

*Let me willingly acknowledge life as I find it (as life is, was or may be) even though I may not approve of what I find, have wisdom to see what would be good to change when following my Leading Principals and values, willingly choose to start, willingly choose to follow through, and be grateful for the opportunity to try to live my life as best I can.*

Many people have heard a prayer that is usually credited to the American theologian Reinhold Niebuhr. A common version of this prayer is: "God grant me the serenity to accept the things I cannot change, courage to change the things I can, and the wisdom to know the difference." The formula offered here takes a different approach to acceptance and change than the approach offered by this prayer. While the prayer limits acceptance only to what cannot be changed, the formula encourages acceptance of all that is, was, or ever may be. Here's why.

Suppose you have a room with a door on one wall. With enough money and effort, you could have that door changed to a different wall. With enough money and effort, it could be done even if you had to tear down and rebuild the entire building to do it. And yet, you could never move the door if you refused to acknowledge that the door is where it is right now: if you kept insisting, "No, it's not there. I refuse to acknowledge life, including the placement of this door, as I have found it!"

That is why this formula starts with willingly acknowledging the world as it is, was or may be regardless of whether the conditions can be changed or not. For the moment, the world is as it is right now, was as it used to be, or may possibly be in the future. We only reduce our ability to change things, even the things we can change, when we refuse to acknowledge them to be as they are, were, or might be or when we acknowledge them grudgingly rather than willingly.

The first phrase in this formula, "Let me willingly acknowledge life as I find it (as life is, was or may be) even though I may not approve of what I find," underlines the difference between approving of what we find in the world, and willingly acknowledging it. The formula could just as well have begun with "Let me accept life as I find it" or "Let me give my permission for life as I find it." All of these words are just saying the same thing in slightly different ways or with slightly different inflections. As we have already seen, we live in a world of sorrow and more, or less, sustaining fulfillments. It is a not the world that we would have picked if we had been allowed to do the picking. On the other hand, arguing with reality doesn't help us deal with it any better. By willingly acknowledging life as we find it, all the pain that comes with those arguments with reality disappears, as if by magic. It isn't magic though. The disappearance of that pain comes directly from choosing to willingly acknowledge the world as we find it, even when we do not approve of what we find.

Consider the next phrase, "wisdom to see what would be good to change." It isn't good to change everything. Some things are better left alone even when it is possible to change them. Are we seeking change in the service of the Leading Principles and values that we have chosen for the Big Picture of our lives, or is it change simply for the convenience of the moment or for the sake of change itself? Where I come from, there are sayings like, "Let sleeping dogs lie," "If it ain't broke, don't fix it," "Pick your battles;" and "There is a time for every purpose under heaven." They all make the same point. Wisdom means sometimes acting and sometimes leaving things alone. Wisdom is recognizing what, in this moment, best serves the Leading Principles and values that make up the Big Picture of our life.

Wisdom asks us to recognize that the trouble with a philosophy of "eat, drink and be merry for tomorrow we die" is tomorrow comes and we aren't dead! Instead, we are left with a big mess to clean up. An alternative philosophy is: "if you plan to be around tomorrow, best act like it today." That is what wisdom asks of us – to view what we do in this place and this moment from a wider and longer-term perspective than right here, right now. It asks us to choose what we do in this moment from the perspective of our Leading Principles and values – from the perspective of the Big Picture that we have chosen to make our life about.

Continuing on, let us consider the next phrase, "willingly choose to start, willingly choose to follow through." As is sometimes said, getting the ball rolling isn't the same thing as keeping the ball rolling. Getting started in the service of Leading Principles and values isn't the same thing as continuing to do so. Getting started, as well as following through, are both important. And willingly choosing to act wisely is not the same thing as demanding that you absolutely must act wisely. Humans are allowed to act narrowly and shortsightedly, or to use another term, foolishly. Foolish actions are an option, a possibility. The Formula for Serenity in Action is about making willing choices, not being pushed around by "HAVE-TO's." In the words of one of my mentors, Albert Ellis, "demanding-ness will land me less than what I really want!"

A few illustrations may be useful to make the meaning of "willingly choose" clearer. Consider, for a moment, people who are afraid to fly in an airplane, ride in a train, or even ride in an automobile. Though afraid, they can be "willing with their feet." Many people who are fearful about these modes of transportation simply won't make use of them. They don't get into airplanes or trains or cars. One might say they are not willing with their body, not willing with their hands, arms, feet, and mouth, or, in short, not willing with their feet.

In addition to being willing or unwilling with one's feet, a person can also be willing, or unwilling, "with their heart," Thus, an individual can take a feared method of transportation and grudgingly tolerate or resign themselves the experience. They don't open their heart to the experience, including the experience of being afraid.

The notion of being willing or unwilling with your heart is not about that big muscle in the middle of your chest and, thus, it is metaphorical when compared to being willing with your feet. When it comes to willing with your feet, you can see people moving their hands, arms, feet, and mouth when they get on, or refuse to get on, an airplane or other form of transportation. Willing with your heart is about what others may not so easily see. Here are some activities that may clarify the point.

### Activity 4: Willing with Your Heart

*Make a fist. Do it right now. Actually make a fist with your hand. You will notice that all it takes to have an open hand when you have made a fist is to stop holding your hand closed. If you stop holding your hand closed, it opens all by itself. To flatten your hand, or extend your fingers, you have to do more. But, if you just stop holding your hand closed, it opens all by itself. Achieving an open hand when you have a clenched fist is not something you do. It is something you stop doing – namely holding your hand closed. So it is when it comes to being willing with your heart. "Opening your heart" is not something you do. It is something you stop doing – namely holding it closed. Willingness, itself, is quite similar. If you want to be willing, just stop being unwilling and willingness appears.*

*Another way to contact "being willing with your heart" was noted earlier. Cup your hands. Actually take a moment and cup your hands. Your cupped hands allow you to hold something in them. If I were to put a feather in you cupped hands, it would be gentle – and, you could hold it gently. But suppose I put a cactus fruit, with its sharp spines sticking out, into your cupped hands. That object would not be gentle – and you still could hold it gently. Being willing with your heart is like that. Sometimes, we experience thoughts, images and bodily sensations that are gentle – and we can hold them gently. Sometimes, we experience thoughts, images and bodily sensations that are anything but gentle – and we can hold them gently too. Willingly choosing with your feet basically means willingly following the Formula for Human Liberation – willingly doing something unpleasant, and willingly refraining from doing something pleasant, in the service of something you make more important. Willingness with your heart means holding gently whatever shows up when you do so.*

Here's a third way to contact willingness. If you have ever gone to a movie, you know you have to pay to go in. There is a price of admission. Where I live, the security at movies is pretty good, so, typically, if you don't pay, you can't go. Life works the same way. If you don't pay by moving your hands, arms, feet, and mouth in certain ways, then there will be places you cannot go. You will not have paid the price of admission.

Now, if you make a rule like, "There are certain thoughts, certain images and certain feelings I refuse to have," then you will find there are certain places your hands, arms, feet, and mouth cannot take you. Why? Because, as soon as they do, the very thoughts, images, and feelings you have a rule about not having suddenly appear. Not only is there a price of admission to be paid with your hands, arms, feet, and mouth, but there is also a price of admission to be paid in thoughts, images, and bodily sensations. As soon as you refuse to pay either part of the "price of admission," you can't go.

And when you get up to the pay booth at the movie, do you scream and curse the person taking the money and throw your price of admission at them. No. You not only pay, you pay willingly. The Formula for Serenity in Action is not about making sure the only thoughts, images, or bodily sensations that show up in your life are one's we might call, "serene." The serenity in this formula is about how you relate to whatever shows up. Will you hold life gently while you act in the service of your Leading Principles and values, or will you get in a fight with life? You can pick. In what direction will you take your spiritual development?

Our world is filled with many instances of "if you don't pay, you can't go." Sometimes these are expressed as "have to's." For example, if we are going to get into the movie, we have to pay. This is what we might call a "contingent relation" between one thing and another: If abc then xyz is required. If we are going to abc then we have to xyz. For example, If I want to open a door but am too far from the door to touch the handle, then I will have to get closer to the door.

Our mind and body may help us identify these contingent relations. However, the spiritual aspect of our being helps us with how we travel through them. And importantly, the truth of contingent relations does not determine how we travel through them. One might say that there are different banners under which one can travel and our experience when we travel one way can be quite different than our experience when we travel another.

*Activity 5: Two Banners*

*Stand far enough from a door that you cannot reach the door handle without moving a little distance. In other words, create a physical contingency such that you have to get closer to the door in order to touch the handle. You are now ready to travel to the door under different banners.*

*The first banner is "I HAVE TO." As you walk over to touch the door handle, say out loud and with as much conviction as you can manage, "I HAVE TO, I HAVE TO, I HAVE TO" for as long as it takes to get to the door. And also travel in a particular way - grudgingly.*

*After traveling to the door under the banner of "I HAVE TO grudgingly," make the trip under the banner of "I CHOOSE TO, I CHOOSE TO, I CHOOSE TO" said out loud and with as much conviction as you can manage for as long as it takes to get to the door. And this time, rather than traveling grudgingly, travel willingly.*

*If this activity worked as imagined, you will have noticed that the contingencies of the universe did not change regardless of how you traveled through them. And, most importantly, you will have found you prefer to travel under "I CHOOSE TO willingly" rather than "I HAVE TO grudgingly," because "I CHOOSE TO willingly" is the life of a spiritually liberated human being while "I HAVE TO grudgingly" is the life of spiritual struggle. No one wants to live life trapped in struggle and if you are doing so, then look out for periodic revolts, "Oh yeah, I HAVE TO! Watch this!"*

*Now make one final trip and, as you are walking, notice that you could immediately turn to the right or to the left or continue toward the door. Depending on what objects are nearby, you might run into something, but you could still make the turn or continue toward the door. In that moment you are in contact with what we might call "Human Freedom." It exists in every moment though we often don't notice it. There is no moment in which we cannot radically alter what we are doing or continue as we are. Said slightly differently, "there is nothing you can do that can't be done!"*

Having addressed the spiritual importance of willingly choosing, let us turn to the last line of the Formula for Serenity in Action, "gratitude for the opportunity to try to live my life as best I can." Human beings can imagine possible futures and then try to bring those possible futures into actual existence. That is how the computer I am using to type these words got invented. Once upon a time, computers were only a possibility. The present now contains actual computers. A possible future was brought into actual existence. The other thing about human beings is that we can set standards for our behavior and then try to meet the standards. The cows and the pigs, and the dogs and the cats are not doing this! When did you see any being, other than a human being, carrying around a set of plans for the future or a set of standards for behavior? We humans seem to be the only ones!

What these plan-making and standard-setting abilities mean is that we have more sorrow than any other beings on the planet. Why? Because failure is common. And, when our plans don't work out, or our behavior doesn't meet the standards we set, sorrow swiftly follows. Even so, I suggest these abilities are something to be grateful for. We seem to be the only ones that can do these things. Every other being on the planet is living its life as best it can. Only we can be said to be *trying* to live our lives as best we can because we are the only ones, as far as we know, that can have these kinds of ends-in-view. We human beings are the only beings we know of that can have Leading Principles which we can willingly choose to follow and values we can willingly carry out when we follow them. And that, I suggest, is something to be grateful for. We are the only ones who can try to live our lives as best we can. The only ones who can adopt the Formula for Serenity in Action.

# Chapter 5
## "WAY COOL"

There is a kind of arbitrariness about spiritual development. Once you wake up to the possibility of picking what your body is in service of, you can pick anything! Spiritual development is about that you pick rather than what you pick. Once you begin picking, all the following aspects of spirituality will be present: imminence (right here right now), infinitude (never used up), transcendence (beyond the present moment), Leading Principles (directions to travel in life) and values (the way or manner we want to travel no matter the direction). It is a little like building strong muscles without regard to the purpose for which those muscles will be put. With strong muscles, you can carry a person across a stream or drown the person in it. Picking directions and then pursuing them are actions that can be done without regard to which directions are picked and pursued. I believe this is why spiritual development can sometimes proceed so weirdly.

For example, for some individuals, spiritual development is aimed at "getting out of life." Being a human being means living with sorrow and more or less sustaining fulfillments. Spiritual development can be put in the service of trying to overcome or get out of that. While it could be put to that pursuit, there is nothing about spiritual development, in and of itself, that requires it proceed in that direction or in any other direction. Spiritual development doesn't have to be put in the service of something like overcoming the basic facts of human existence or somehow getting out of life and its sorrows. Thus, what I offer below is not the only way to development spiritually. It is one way. A way you could choose but you don't have to choose.

If you try different things in your life, you may have an experience that will be like hearing one instrument playing softly. And, that instrument and that music will, somehow, produce a sort of echo within you. It will be as if you are a kind of tuning fork so that when a particular note is struck, the same note resonates within you. And, if you follow that music, it may fade away because, sometimes, it is an illusion.

By which I mean something that seems one way but turns out to be a different way. On the other hand, the music may grow louder.

And another instrument joins in. And, after continuing this pursuit, you may find you are resonating to what seems the sound a whole orchestra playing in more than one musical style.

If you try to talk to someone about this, you will find that about the only thing you can really say is that the experience is just "WAY COOL." It is really beyond the ability of words to adequately describe. You might say "beautiful," or "sublime" or "deeply fulfilling" but no words really seem adequate. Even if you are able to produce for another person the music that moves you, they may well respond with, "That? That is what you are trying to tell me about? You must be kidding!"

And, if you find someone who is moved by the same, or similar, music that is moving you, then, while you may be able to have long conversations about that music, each conversation has to end with nothing more than mutual smiles of acknowledgement. Even for those who move to the same or similar music, there are just no adequate words. It's just WAY COOL.

Once, while visiting a zoo, I was standing by an enclosure for lions. There was a stream running through the enclosure and while I was there, some insects began emerging from the water. Each popped through the surface and rode the current just long enough for its wings to dry, and then took flight. Although some distance away, a lioness took notice, almost from the emergence of the first insect. She walked over, plopped down, and stayed transfixed until the insect hatch was over. She didn't come to eat the insects or protect herself from them. As far as I could tell, it was for her, and for me, just WAY COOL!

Consider bird watching. What's the point? All that happens is that you see some birds. It doesn't put food on the table. It won't keep you warm when it's cold or cool when it's hot. It has no use! And yet, some people will spend lots of money and time doing it. Why? For them, it's just WAY COOL.

On the other hand, WAY COOL might turn out to be putting food on the table or staying warm when it's cold or cool when it's hot. Those looking from the outside may conclude what is moving the person is simply the practical requirements of existing or existing more comfortably. And yet, that person finds those activities to be just WAY COOL.

The important thing to be noticed is that WAY COOL can't be determined by anyone but the individual. It doesn't have to be any particular way or any particular thing. It is whatever resonates with you and no one can really know that except you! It is the kind of fulfillment that makes you not only glad to be alive but seems like the essence of living. It is human life connected to that "buzz of being," even though it is the same human life that brings human sorrows. You may experience a sense of gratitude for getting the chance to experience such fulfillment. You have the sense of life transforming from merely existing until you die to really living! And from the perspective presented here, that opportunity is available right here, right now rather than at some distant time and place.

At the time of single celled organisms dividing in two to make more like themselves, there was but one rule. We might call it "The Rule of Life" - stay alive long enough to make more like me. As life developed it required connection between two individuals to bring new life into the world. For these organisms the Rule of Life became to stay alive long enough to make more like us. For fish that might be staying alive long enough to have fertilized eggs in a streambed of clean gravel. Nothing further is included. For some fish, it takes two or three years from fertilized egg to producing fertilized eggs. For humans, it takes a lot longer and there is a lot more is included!

The point is that neither mere physical existence nor The Rule of Life, stay alive long enough to make more like us, is what is meant by really living, even if you must first physically exist to really live. That sense of aliveness beyond mere physical existence is about being in contact with, what is for you, WAY COOL, something truly mysterious, something beyond words and, yet, not beyond the possibility of human experience. It is something utterly personal. Others may offer suggestions or clues but, in the end, only you can say if that echo or that resonance is within you. And yet, it is not uniquely personal. A great many individuals may be moving, in concert, to their own variations of the same symphony that first began by each following a single echo. Their coordinated efforts extend, broaden, and deepen the music.

Not only can we light up with experiences that are beyond words to describe, but we are also capable of noticing others who are lit up in that same way, even if not by the same thing. We see they are somehow really alive rather than merely existing. They are doing more than simply making more like them. They seem to be, at least at certain times if not all the time, fully awake while so many others seem to be sleeping. And, in some strange way, it is rousing to be with others who are awake and no longer just sleep walking though one routine after another. The Greek sages would not have advised those around them to "know thyself" if either doing so didn't make an important difference in a person's time on earth, or if everyone were already doing it.

Consider what happens when humans actually listen to music. They often find that there is certain music that, quite literally, gets them moving. Their toes tap. Their head bob. Their body sways. I have seen such movement in auditoriums where orchestras are playing classical nineteenth century European music and in bar rooms where sound systems play the United States brand of Country and Western music. Some people find themselves moved by lots of different types of music and some people are moved by only one type, or even only one piece of music. The point is, when that swept up moment happens, you know it. You can fight back. You can make sure you don't let your toes tap, your head bob or your body sway. You can try to make sure others don't see or even try not to notice yourself. And yet, the very act of trying to control yourself is evidence that you are already being moved.

What I have been attempting to talk about are an individual's most sustaining fulfillments. They are that which we not only desire but that which we most deeply desire. They are not merely pleasant in the moment, if they are pleasant in the moment. They are sustaining in some way that doesn't seem to be just about sustaining your body and/or your mind even though they are deeply grounded in your bones and blood. They are that over which, if you pursue them, you will be forced to risk your deepest sorrows. Why?

Because they are your deepest desires, and life does not guarantee that you will ever even make contact with the deepest fulfillment of those deepest desires or be able to sustain that fulfillment once you do. On the other hand, neither does life guarantee that you will not be able to build a symphony of living, rather than just existing until you die while, possibly and additionally, following the Rule of Life and making more like us in the meantime.

Despite the risk of enormous pain, and the certainty of sometimes actually experiencing it, these deepest desires are what can energize us even when there is no rational, logical, or sensible reason to our being energized by them and when neither we, nor anyone else, understands or can explain that power. This is why I have been careful not to use phrases like "the world talking to you," or "the world telling you something." The very nature of talk is making sense. And WAY COOL is not about sense-making at all. What resonates with you is what resonates with you. That it is rational, logical or makes sense has nothing to do with it.

There is nothing about the spiritual aspect of our being that requires us to pick the pursuit of our deepest desires. We don't have to pursue our WAY COOL, instead of something else. We are just as capable of picking the denial of our deepest desires as we are capable of picking their pursuit. It is from your spiritual center that you can make your toes, your head and any other part of your body be still. And yet, it is also from your spiritual center that you could pick acting in the service of your deepest desires if that is that direction you choose to move. You don't have to dance the music that moves you – and you could willingly choose to.

Many people find they haven't gotten much instruction about WAY COOL. They have not been encouraged to try things and listen for the echo inside you. Or, because the echo can turn out to be an illusion, indeed that first instrument playing softly sometimes does fade away, individuals are told it is always an illusion – that it will always fade away. Such pursuits are said to be a waste of time, idealistic nonsense, not serious, or perhaps for a special few but certainly not you! If individuals try to talk to others about their new experience in the shallows of what for them is WAY COOL, they may have been told, "Pay no attention to that."

Instead, they have often been told to get on a path. They are given a life agenda to follow. Agreeing with the American mythologist Joseph Campbell, I suggest that if you follow a path, you can be sure it is someone else's path. Yes, we all start as children and, if we live long enough, the powers that come with having grown up will begin to wane. Human life does have that sort of arc, from birth to death. Nevertheless, whatever moment you are in, it is a moment that you have never been in before. If you look backwards in your life, there is a path because you made it. If you look forward, there is no path, unless someone else has made it. This is the point of Leading Principles and values. Leading Principles give you direction in the wilderness that every moment actually is, no matter how familiar that moment seems. None of us have ever been in this moment before, nor will we be again. Values give you ways, or manners, to move in that direction. There have been many human lives lived, but not yours. You are the only one that can do it! You are the only one who can live your life. Have you picked your Leading Principles and values, or are you operating half asleep off an agenda someone else handed you, maybe a long time ago?

Following someone else's agenda is a common way to what some call a mid-life crisis. You get to the top of the ladder and find it's against the wrong wall! If you are unsuccessful at mid-life, you can still hold out hope. "If I could just get up there." You may be disappointed, but you won't yet have the crisis that comes when you find you've arrived and it's no place you actually care to be. It turns out that after all the time and effort you spent, there's no there, there!

To repeat, there is nothing about spiritual development that requires you, or anyone else, to connect your Leading Principles and values to WAY COOL. You are completely free to develop spiritually in connection with activities entirely unrelated to, or in total conflict with, your deepest desires. You can take that agenda you have been handed and follow it to the letter until your dying day. You will still be able to use the Formulas for Human Liberation and Serenity in Action. And that's the spiritual point. There is nothing you can do that can't be done – including giving no time at all to that which most deeply moves you. The choice is utterly and completely up to you.

However, the remainder of this book is written with the aim of serving those who choose to connect WAY COOL with their spiritual development. If you choose this approach, then, by picking your Leading Principles and values, your life will have direction even though there will be no path except the one behind you.

*Activity 6: End of the Day Reflection*

*At the end of each day reflect on the experiences of that day with this question, "Was there anything I did today that, looking back on it, was actually worth my time?" Notice that the question is not "was it fun" or "did I have a good time." At the time, it may not have been that pleasant at all. The key factor is that, on reflection, and for you, it was worth having done. Make a record of your answer. Do this every day for at least a month. If, after at least a month of keeping these records, you find that you have done very little that, on reflection at the end of each day, was worth the time you spent doing it, then add this question: "What would I willingly do tomorrow (doing it unwillingly doesn't count), that I don't usually do or have never done?" By following through with your answer, you will have one new thing to consider when answering the first question at the end of each day.*

This simple but systematic way of listening for, and keeping track of, what actually resonates or echoes within you on a day-to-day basis can begin to give you a sense of what WAY COOL might be for you and allows you to planfully pursue whatever it turns out to be, thus allowing you to have more and more of it in your life.

# Chapter 6
## Life as an Exciting Adventure

As we have seen, life is risky. Every moment of life contains the possibility of sorrow, the experience we have when we don't get what we want or do get what we don't want. Much more than we would wish, potential sorrow becomes actual sorrow. With enough sorrow, tears come out of our eyes, cries come out of our throat, snot comes out of nose and our entire body shakes – an experience that can be so powerful that it sometimes feels like we can't survive it, even though we do. And though life has many fulfillments that are more like cotton candy than sustaining vegetables, we also can choose to pursue what for us is WAY COOL when picking Leading Principles and values that give us directions to travel and ways to travel in those directions. Developing spiritually in this way is more than just surviving for a long time in comfortable conditions before we finally die. Living spiritually in this way is about adventures.

Adventures have at least two aspects. First, you cannot know for sure how it is going to turn out. If you go on a ride at an amusement park, you are not on an adventure. Everyone knows how the ride ends. Quite often you sit down on the very seats from which you just saw the previous riders exit. Being at the top of a "Ferris wheel" or riding a roller coaster may be exciting. You may even have a sense of danger. But it isn't really an adventure – you know how it ends. Jumping off a one-story building is an adventure. Maybe you break your leg. Maybe you walk away. Jumping off a ten-story building isn't an adventure. You know how that ends.

Second, there must be some sense of danger. If there is no sense of danger, we call it "a walk in the park." If you go ambling in the park, you may not know in advance where the walk will end, so it does fulfill the first requirement. However, without a sense of danger, it's not an adventure. It remains just a walk in the park, a phrase that differentiates a pleasant way to pass time from an adventure.

Sometimes we choose to do something when we are uncertain about the outcome, and we have a sense of danger. These are cases of choosing an adventure. At other times, life simply launches us on one. Instead of a sense of having chosen, we have a sense that, "it just happened." If you suddenly have a sense of danger and the realization that you don't know how things are going to turn out, nothing is wrong. You are simply realizing that you are on an adventure, even if it is an adventure that you didn't choose.

The truth is, we are always taking risks. Even when we don't have a sense of danger, but instead feel safe, we never really know for sure if we are in danger or not. Though we often think we know how things will turn out, we actually don't possess that kind of foreknowledge. Even amusement park rides have been known to have accidents – outcomes that were neither intended nor anticipated. Life can, and does, surprise us. Stuff happens! We can, and do, unknowingly take risks, but it is awareness that turns them into adventures.

If you want to ruin an adventure novel, you immediately turn to the back of the book and read the last thirty, or so, pages. The whole point of an adventure novel is to experience the uncertainty of not knowing how the novel will turn out as well as a sense of danger along the way. However, if you are now reading these words, you are still writing the story of your own life. You can't turn to the back of the book and learn how it all turns out. Granted, we all know the very last line is, "and then I die," but we can't say for sure what comes before that moment or what ripple effects continue on after our life ends.

Spiritual development, from the perspective presented here, is finding that which for you is WAY COOL and picking Leading Principles and values to aid in its pursuit in a context of sorrow and death. Lean on the possibility that you might fail, and you will have a sense of danger. Lean on the possibility that you might succeed, and you will have a sense of excitement. Lean on both and you will have a sense of danger and excitement. It is this possibility of life as an exciting adventure that the words I have written are intended to point. Your alarm system is often activated, even if only slightly, because that is what happens when you have a sense of danger. You realize, in the moment, that stuff you don't want to happen might happen or stuff you do want to happen might not.

However, the spiritual aspect of your being allows you to be at the "eye of the hurricane" even as the winds around the eye blow very strongly. Developing spiritually means cultivating your ability to be at the stable place at the center of the storm, rather than trying to ensure there are never any storms. Are you experiencing the sensations that come from the activation of your alarm system when on an exciting adventure? Certainly! And when you are at the spiritual eye of a hurricane, the place from which you can experience those sensations as nothing more or less than strong, even very strong sensations, your relationship with them is different than when you are out on the edge of the hurricane spinning with them. Developing spiritually is being able to make that shift from the edge to the center.

The spiritual aspect of your being is a place from which you can choose to be on an exciting adventure – an activity that is full of possibility, including both the possibility of sorrow AND fulfillment. You "don't know" and yet you go. It is from your spiritual center that you can both choose to go on exciting adventures filled with possibility and also choose to go willingly rather than go grudgingly or with some other form of unwilling engagement. With the spiritual aspect of your being, you can take your thoughts and feelings with you even if in some sense they don't want to go or actively protest. Often, if your mind and body are well developed, they can become excellent servants when exciting adventures are formulated as possible choices and when you are actually living them.

Sailing ships are said to have an attitude. They literally tilt in a particular direction. This notion of the tilt of your exciting adventure ship can serve as a useful metaphor. I suggest the most useful attitude with which to proceed, is one of let's see rather than I, or we, know. "Let's see" helps you stay awake to the many possibilities contained in every moment, possibilities that may change from one moment to the next moment and that you may not have even considered when you began. "I know" can lead you to overlook these newly revealed possibilities. Your Leading Principles and values help you further refine this process because they help you keep a sharp eye out for subtle, but important, changes you might otherwise miss.

Here is a possibility to consider. What if, for you, choosing to willingly live exciting adventures with an attitude of let's see turned out to be WAY COOL? As suggested elsewhere, you are the only one who can actually answer this question no matter how many others try to answer it for you. And, you have all that is required to produce that answer. From your spiritual center you can develop your skill of noticing as well as noticing that you are noticing. You can develop your skill of picking both the direction and the way or manner you move your hands, arms, feet, and mouth. You can move to the eye of the hurricane, even as the winds of danger and uncertainty are blowing strongly around it. With these skills you can try choosing to willingly live an exciting adventure with an attitude of "let's see" and find out if, for you, approaching life in this way is, indeed, WAY COOL.

# Chapter 7
## Getting Centered & Reducing Tension

Since we are all going to live lives that include thoughts, images, and bodily sensations, it is important to both make them work for our spiritual development when we can and willingly ignore them when we cannot.

**Centering**

An audio version of Activity 7 below can be found on YouTube. It is titled "Centering and Tension Reduction Exercise by Hank Robb." However, if you would like to create your own, or read it to someone else, the basic text is below. I call it "centering" because the point of the activity is to center yourself in the moment in which you are actually living and also because it is an activity done from your spiritual center. I encourage doing this activity for about ten minutes as part of your routine to prepare for your day. Likely you wash your face, brush your teeth, or do other things to get ready for the day. Since you are going to have lots of thoughts, images, and bodily sensations all day long, you might as well get ready for them too. And by developing this skill, you can use it throughout the day whenever it might prove helpful.

*Activity 7: Centering*

*Begin by noticing the way the furniture and the floor are supporting your body. You may notice that I did not begin by saying, "Make yourself comfortable" or some similar statement. There is nothing wrong with being comfortable and that is not what this activity is about. This activity is about being psychologically present in the moment you are actually in whether you are comfortable in that moment or not. So, begin by noticing the bodily sensations you experience from the support your body is receiving from any furniture, floor or ground that supports you, or even from your own body if other parts of your body are resting there.*

*You will likely find that you experience a variety of sensations, with the ones from the floor or ground being quite firm and others being less so. Regardless of the differences in these sensations, you have a variety of ways you might relate to them. One of these ways is to make efforts to change or alter your sensations. Just move around a little and your sensations will change. ... An alternative way to contact your bodily sensations of support is to notice them simply as they are, without efforts to change or alter them. That is what I invite you to do ... for just a moment or two ... here and now (continue noticing for a few moments).*

*Though your bodily sensations of support are rather static, the two alternative ways of relating to bodily sensations can be used with more dynamic sensations like the coming and going of your breath. You really don't have to do anything. Air arrives and departs all by itself. As air enters your body, your chest rises. As air leaves your body, your chest falls. Your belly moves in a coordinated way with the rising and falling of your chest.*

*While you don't have to do anything for air to enter and leave your body, there are things you could do. As before, you could make efforts to change or alter the experience. You could make yourself breathe a little more rapidly or a little more slowly. And, as before, you also could choose to notice the coming and going of your breath simply as it is, ... without any efforts to change or alter it. ... So, for just a moment, I invite you to make that second choice of just noticing the experience. Breath comes and goes at its own rate and with its own rhythm and you can contact that experience simply as it is ... here and now ... for just a moment or two (continue noticing for a few moments).*

*These same alternatives are available with other dynamic experiences like the coming and going of your thoughts and images. By thoughts, I mean those "radio programs" inside your head. By images, I mean anything with a picture. It could be a still picture, a moving picture, or a moving picture with sound.*

*Just as before, you could make efforts to alter or change your thoughts and images. There is also that second alternative. The choice to notice thoughts and images simply as they are: thoughts as collections of sounds ... and images as collections of shapes and colors.*

*And, if you make that choice, you may begin to notice how often thoughts and images invite you to go, psychologically, traveling ... to some other place or time. You are invited to leave this moment for some other moment ... and to leave this place for some other place. And yet, even though you are invited to go psychologically traveling, you could choose to remain here – in this moment and in this place.*

*It's a little like sitting at a taxicab stand. A cab pulls up. The door opens. And there's a thought or an image ... inviting you to get in and go traveling. Inviting you to leave here and now ... and travel to then and there. And though invited to go traveling, you could choose to remain here, in this place, and now, in this moment. And if you just sit noticing the thought or image simply as it is, then, in a while, the door closes. The cab leaves. Another arrives. Another door opens ... and another thought or image invites you to get in ... and go, psychologically, traveling. And if, once again, you remain seated, just noticing the thought or image simply as it is, then, after a while, that door closes. ... And that cab leaves. ... And another arrives. And so on. And so on. And so on.*

*And should you find that you have gone psychologically traveling, even without intending to do so, once you notice it, you could immediately return to this moment and this place ... simply by choosing to do so. ... And, by making that choice, make available a wide variety of experiences that are right here, right now ... including the coming and going of your breath ... and the way your body is supported by the furniture and the floor.*

*So, when you have that sense of being right here, right now, as present psychologically as you are physically, in this moment and this place, then you have achieved the point of this activity and you are ready to move on to the next thing in your life.*

**Some Reflections on Centering**

There are a couple of things to notice about this centering activity, especially after the first time you do it. First, you may notice you became more relaxed. Most people have that experience. And you may notice that there was nothing about becoming "relaxed" in what you read or heard. All that you were asked to do was become psychologically present in the moment you were actually in.

When thoughts, images and bodily sensations are contacted as nothing more, and nothing less, than thoughts, images, and bodily sensations there is nothing dangerous about them, and so, we tend to relax.

This relaxing gives a little clue about how often in life we have gone psychologically traveling to some place or time that does seem dangerous and so we find our mind and body "ready for action." Though many people close their eyes during this activity, there was no instruction to do so. With your eyes open, you saw what was immediately around you. If there was nothing dangerous around you, then being directly in contact with an environment containing no danger also contributed to you becoming more relaxed. However, if there had been something dangerous in your environment, then all the more reason to be psychologically present because being psychologically present in the moment we are actually in enhances our ability to deal with that moment. Relaxation is often a side effect of centering, but relaxation is not the point of centering. The point of the activity is to be psychologically present in the moment you are actually in whether relaxed or not. Even so, it can be useful to reduce tension and below is a second activity designed for that purpose.

**Tension Reduction**

An audio version of Activity 8 below is the second half of the YouTube recording called "Centering and Tension Reduction Exercise by Hank Robb." Sometimes it can be useful to make efforts to change or alter experience, including bodily tension. Without some bodily tension, you would fall down or fall over. However, there is really no reason to carry around more bodily tension than is required for living in the moment you are actually in, and bodily tension often seems to creep in without our awareness. Activity 8 below is a method to both reduce all the bodily tension that can be reduced and also carry the remainder gently.

*Activity 8: Tension Reduction*

*Though it is not necessary, most people find it useful to close their eyes in this activity. Begin at the top of your head and let your attention drift toward the tips of your fingers and the tips of your toes looking for places of bodily tension.*

*When you find the first one, notice that it is made up of two parts. You seem to have some control over one part of the tension, no matter how large or small that part may be. Over the other you do not. The part over which you have some control may be less than one percent or more than fifty percent. However large or small, it is tension you could release, or dismiss, or let go, or turn loose of, and I invite you to do so. Taking note of your ability to hold any*

42

*experience gently whether that experience is gentle or not, I invite*
*you to hold the remaining tension gently as you move on to the next*
*place in your body where you are experiencing tension. When you*
*arrive there, respond as before. First, find the portion of this tension*
*over which you seem to have some control. Whether the portion of*
*tension over which you have some control is small or large, proceed*
*by releasing, or dismissing, or letting go, or turning loose of that*
*portion of the tension. Hold the remainder gently and proceed on to*
*the next place of tension repeating the process of letting go and*
*holding gently until you have arrived at the tips of your fingers and*
*the tips of your toes.*

### Reflections on Tension Reduction Activity

Many individuals are surprised at how much tension they are
able to release the first time they go through this process. Others find
they are not able to release much tension at all. Almost everyone
reports that, with practice, they can increase their ability to release
tension through this method. There is no virtue in carrying around a
lot of excess tension, so an activity aimed at reducing it can be
useful. It is important to note that the tension reduction activity
described above directly aims at reducing tension while centering
only does so as a side effect. So, use the tension reduction activity if
you aim to reduce physical tension and the centering activity to
develop your ability to be more psychologically present in the
moment you are actually in.

# Chapter 8
## Good Servants, Poor Masters

Long before I showed up on this planet, someone noticed that human minds make good servants but poor masters. This is an important piece of wisdom for spiritual development because our mind, even more often than our body, clamors to be our master rather than our servant. Minds are sense-making organs, and we might say, they are so proud of their abilities that they continually insist their abilities be placed at the "top of the heap" rather than in the service of something else.

Let us, for a moment, consider "sense-making," itself. If I were to claim that most cars made in the United States of America are manufactured in New York City, the claim would be factually wrong. Even so, the sentence would "make sense," at least to someone who "speaks English." The words would "hang together" in the way the following group of words does not, "Green rampantly up frog lawn over before." Each of those words is recognizable as an "English word." But put together as they are, they don't "make sense." They don't "hang together." The words don't "cohere," and so we don't have a "coherent sentence."

Human beings are communicators. And, we learn quite early that simply stringing sounds, or gestures, together, even if they are "the words of our language" simply won't do. We have to organize the words of our language in a way that "makes sense" if words are to work with our mom or dad or brother or sister or neighbor or whomever we are "talking to." From very early in our lives, everyone around us makes "sense-making" very important. And, it isn't long before we make it important too. It is one thing to be "wrong." It is a very different thing not even to "make sense."

If we don't pay careful attention, sense-making easily becomes more important than anything else. We begin insisting that everything "make sense." We refuse to tolerate experiences in our lives that don't "make sense." We insist on "knowing the reason" (another way of "making sense") for this or that no matter what the this or that is. We insist that all the aspects of life "hang together."

This is why our spiritual development can run into conflict with our mind, our sense-making organ. Spiritual development is about picking what you make important. And, picking what you make important doesn't require that what you make important "make sense" either before, or after, you pick it. In fact, the whole act of living life by particular Leading Principles and values simply by choosing to live life the way you choose makes no "sense" whatsoever. "Where is the REASON that you pick this rather than that?" your mind may insist. And yet, there doesn't have to be a reason for your pick even if your mind insists there must be. You can just "pick." You can pick living life in the service of WAY COOL, but you could just as well pick living life in the service of something else. There is nothing more or less "reasonable" or "sensible" about picking WAY COOL than there is in picking anything else. And so, minds rebel. "Make sense! Make sense! Make sense! None of this nonsense of not making sense!" your mind may scream. In fact, it may be screaming that right now.

Exercising your ability to simply pick what you make your life about may seem utterly crazy to your mind and exposes an underlying aspect of "making sense." Namely, you already have to be up to something before you can sensibly apply sense-making.

Long before sense-making showed up, all life was living consistent with what we might call The Rule of Life: live long enough to make more like you/us. And early on, the living beings we call human beings applied sense-making to that. They didn't have to "find a point" to which they could apply their sense-making ability. They ALREADY had one, just as do all other life forms. However, the spiritual aspect of our being means we don't have to apply our sense-making ability only to the Rule of Life. We can apply it to ANYTHING we pick. But picking what we are going to apply sense-making to has to come first! We can't "sensibly" apply our sense-making ability until we ALREADY have something to apply it to.

If you have already picked the activity indicated by the words "eat ice cream," then it "makes sense" to find out where you can get ice cream and go there. It "makes sense" to find out how much it will cost to get the ice cream, somehow obtain what it will cost, and be ready to pay when you get to where the ice cream is. Now everything "hangs together." Finding out where you can get ice cream and then going there doesn't "make sense" if you haven't already chosen to eat ice cream. Without already having a point, no activity can "make sense."

It can be informative to watch this process in reverse. Life happens and the individuals insist that what happened "make sense."

They often weave quite detailed and very interesting stories that "make sense" of what has happened. They may take the basic facts of desire, sorrow, and more or less sustaining fulfillments and weave a story to make sense of these facts: a story that tells us *why* and then a story about that, and then another story about that.

Many individuals are quite distraught when they don't have a story they find satisfying about why things have happened as they have, or a satisfying story about why things are as they are or might be. In the place that I come from, it is not uncommon to hear people say, "Everything happens for a reason" even when we don't know what that "reason" is. I take that way of speaking about life to be yet another example of how insistent we are about sense-making. That life simply is as it is for NO REASON at all is a very unsatisfactory state of affairs for almost all minds. And so, the sense-making begins, or begins again.

This is a tricky thing about "spiritual development." Spiritual development begins when you realize that YOU CAN PICK and proceeds by you actually picking, over and over and over again. You learn to move from your "spiritual center" regardless of how your mind or body responds to you doing so. And you begin realizing how often you have moved in this way or that in your life without much "picking" having gone on at all. You were simply on "automatic pilot."

As you develop spiritually, you realize things don't HAVE TO "feel good" or "make sense" in order for you to pick them even if your body and mind insist that they do. And you also realize that neither do things HAVE TO "feel bad" or be "nonsensical" in order for you to pick them. Things don't HAVE TO be any *particular* way for you to PICK. You can just PICK. Your mind would have you first do what your mind does best, namely "makes sense," before you do anything else just as your body will be inclined to move toward what "feels good" and away from what "feels bad." Ask your mind, "What is my most important organ" and it will almost certainly answer, "Your mind of course!" And where did that opinion come from?

Even so, your body and mind are not your enemies when it comes to spiritual development. They can be very useful servants. Your body can help you sense what is most likely to work in the moment you are actually in when it comes to following your Leading Principles and values even without "thinking about it." Such moments are often described with words such as, "I just sensed what to do," or "I acted on intuition" rather than, "I considered the options."

Your mind not only can help you in the moment, but it can help you coordinate behavior in the service of your Leading Principles and values over extensive periods of time, even decades. With a well-developed mind, you can often "think things through" in a way that is very helpful in following your Leading Principles and values. There is nothing wrong with developing and maintaining a strong mind and strong body. I can't actually imagine when it wouldn't be very useful to do so. Strong servants will be more valuable than weak ones. The point is that developing spiritually requires acting WITH your mind and body and FROM your spiritual center rather than acting FROM your mind or body while the spiritual aspect of your being just comes along for the ride.

# Chapter 9
## Eternity and Unity

"Eternity" and "unity" are being discussed together because the experience of time dropping away and the experience of underlying unity in a universe of apparent division are two experiences that often are given special status when people talk about spiritual development.

## Eternity

Using the sense-making abilities provided by our mind, we human beings have invented many, many ways to "make sense" of ourselves, other people, and the world around us. One of those ways involves framing experience from the perspective of time. The time perspective allows us to formulate plans. "This," whatever the "this" is, comes first, then "that," whatever the "that" is, comes next and then "this other" comes after "that." And so, we "make plans about the future." Looking "backwards" with the time perspective, we can "understand" or "make sense" of our "past." First "this" happened, and then "that" happened, and then "this other" thing happened. Using this particular kind of sense-making we call "time," we can relate to things as happening in the past, in the present or in the future. We can differentiate "now" from "then," whether "then" is "before-now" or "after-now."

One way we use the word "eternity" indicates a long time. So much time that time never runs out – an infinite amount of time.

However, if we consider time as just one more sense-making activity, the word "eternity" can designate experiences where the sense-making activity of time stops. We get little glimpses of such experiences when we have been so deeply involved in an activity like having a conversation, reading a book, or cultivating a garden that we suddenly say or think something like, "Oh! Look how late it has gotten! Where did the time go?!"

It is not that these experiences lasted a long, long time. Instead, while we were engaged in them, the sense-making activity of framing experience from the perspective of time simply dropped away. We might say that we were simply and fully, "living in the moment" rather than making sense of it through one of the many ways our mind has of making sense, in this case, time. If we take this view, then spiritually speaking, an "eternal moment" is not a moment that lasts a long time. It is a moment where one of our mind's many sense-making ways, in this case framing experience from the perspective of time, has dropped away.

## Unity

"Dividing things up" is the foundation of sense making. Here are just a few examples of dividing things up: me and you, my arm and my foot, your clothes and your dwelling, up and down, good and bad, left and right, before and after. Because minds are so good at this, making such divisions can go on and on and on. Very likely there are not enough pages available for me to write down all the ways our minds can give us for dividing things up – including dividing our mind from our body from our spirit. As I noted earlier, our minds can be very, very good servants. This ability to divide things in this way or that way, or a zillion other ways, can turn out to be very helpful, depending on the use to which we put our mind.

However, once again there is an illusion that often goes unnoticed. The illusion is that whatever way we divide the world in any given moment, that way is sensed to be *in the world itself*, rather than the result of our mind's activity. On such occasions when this dividing behavior stops, the illusion breaks, and we get a very different experience. Rather than a universe filled with division, we get the sense of unity that, somehow, always was, and always is, "there" or "underlying" these multitudes of divisions. This experience of unity, oneness, or wholeness can be stunning and, quite literally, breathtaking. That is one reason individuals may ingest certain substances to produce it. This experience of unity, oneness, or wholeness is difficult to speak more clearly about or to give actual concrete examples. This is what inspired the saying, "Those who say, do not know. Those who know, cannot say."

However inexplicable, this experience of unity also can be followed by problems. These are the same problems that showed up with WAY COOL because people often find the experience of unity to be WAY COOL. Talk, talk, talk about ice cream on your tongue and the talk is never the experience of ice cream on your tongue. And talking, talking, talking *about* the stopping of our mind's dividing the world in this way or that, if only momentarily, with the resulting experience of unity, oneness or wholeness cannot capture the actual experience. Words are simply inadequate. Even so, human beings can have such experience – some folks more than others – and some folks more often than others.

When individuals try to talk about this experience that cannot be very well talked about, they end up saying things like, "Well it's one AND many," or "If you've had the experience, you cannot really talk about it," or maybe, "It was just WAY COOL and that's about all I can say." Alternatively, it might have been inexplicably terrifying – the key aspect being "inexplicable." It just doesn't "make sense."

## Eternity and Unity

However, much we find experiences of eternity and unity to be WAY COOL and wish we had more of them in our lives, we get tripped up when our minds, once again, go to work with sense-making. Suddenly, these experiences are supposed to "mean something." They are supposed to mean something even though they are the direct result – in the first instance – of the meaning machine going silent with the kind sense-making we call "time," and in the second instance, with sense-making stopping all together, if only for a moment. Yet, that aspect of our being that we can call "our mind" continues with, "make sense, make sense, MAKE SENSE!" While, from the spiritual aspect of our being, we can simply ignore the question, the result of that spiritual move is very often a mind going into high gear with, "What does it mean?" "What does it mean?" "WHAT DOES IT MEAN?!"

So, here's a little caution I take from Joseph Campbell, "Are you looking for the meaning of life, or the experience of being alive?"

All the sense-making in the world about ice cream, whether it be in the form of thoughts or images, spoken words or written ones, moving pictures or static ones, is not the experience of putting ice cream on your tongue. All the sense-making that can be done will not substitute for WAY COOL experiences, including the WAY COOL of the "eternal moment" or "underlying unity." And that's true even if sense-making, itself, is another instance of experience that individuals find WAY COOL, as it sometimes is for me, and so many others. Rather than pursuing the *meaning* of WAY COOL as your mind will so persistently insist that you do, you could, instead, focus on *experiencing* it. Though you don't HAVE TO pick *pursuing the experience of being alive*, you could!

# Chapter 10
## Habits

Habits are things we do quickly and easily and without much awareness. Acting out of habit is just a fact of life. There is nothing particularly wrong with behaving this way. However, sometimes the actions we take out of habit don't fit very well with the Big Picture we have chosen for our life. Since we quite literally start our life long before we "know what we are doing," it is not surprising that we have developed some habitual actions that don't fit, or no longer fit, with our Leading Principles and values.

For example, if you grow up in a place where people drive on the right-hand side of the road, you will habitually look to your left as you step into the street because that is the direction from which the traffic comes. However, if you find yourself in a place where people drive on the left-hand side of the road, it is best to look to your right as you step into the road because that is now the direction from which traffic comes. Unfortunately, your habit will be to look in what is now the wrong direction. It is "wrong" because conditions have changed. Traffic now comes from the opposite direction. Thus, it would be best to change that habit. Though our mind can help us recognize that changing our habit would be the wise thing to do, habit change actually relies on the spiritual aspect of our being.

As noted, habits are done quickly and easily *and without much awareness*. Thus, changing a habit first requires that we become more aware. It requires "consciousness raising," or noticing, and noticing is a feature of the spiritual aspect of our being. At the outset of habit change, our noticing almost always comes too late. We begin by noticing, "that *didn't* work." In other words, the opportunity to act differently than our habitual way of acting has already passed. Life has moved on. We might recognize, "that didn't work," three months, three weeks, three days, three hours or three minutes later and in each of these cases, the opportunity for different action has come and gone. In such moments, and particularly after we have "done it again," we commonly promise ourselves, "Next time I'll act differently!"

It would be nice if we could immediately change, if we could immediately move from noticing too late to noticing that we are *about* to do the "old thing" so that we could instead do a "new thing." Unfortunately, it commonly doesn't work that way. Instead of going directly from "the-time-for-the-new-behavior-is-past" to "the-time-for-the-new-behavior-is-about-to-be-present," we instead find ourselves in between. By working to raise our awareness, we now notice that though we have already begun our habit, the situation is not yet over. We are aware that we are looking left but only have one foot in the street, so to speak, rather than having already crossed over to the other side.

This process is helped by *slowing down*. Habits are not only done without much awareness, but quickly and easily. When it comes to speed and effectiveness, we can either be quickly or slowly effective, or quickly or slowly ineffective. Habits come quickly and the point of changing our behavior is that the particular habit in which we are interested isn't that effective. So, by slowing down, we give ourselves more time, and thus a better chance, to act more effectively.

Slowing down helps whether we are working to raise awareness or changing our behavior. "What's going on *right here, right now*?" Answering that question requires raising our awareness because we can't "know what's going on right here, right now" and stay on automatic pilot. Slowing down provides time to ask the question and raise our awareness enough to get an answer. It is the way to help address the "without much awareness" aspect of a habit, by providing the time required to become more aware of what we are doing, and what we are experiencing, right here, right now.

Raising our awareness allows us to catch ourselves in the moment of doing the habit and provides our first real opportunity for change. This is the time when we can switch to a "new thing" rather than continuing the "old thing." We can, so to speak, pull our foot from the street and switch from the old automatic pilot habitual action of looking left to the new and different action of looking right – a change that can become the first move in building a habit that better fits our new circumstances.

Then, since we do our habit quickly, slowing down also provides time to recognize, or recall, behavior that fits with our Leading Principles and values and then act in that new way. Slowing down gives us the time we require to act more effectively than provided by our current quick-but-ineffective habit.

If we ask our mind what possible new actions would be consistent with the Big Picture of what we want our life to be about, rather than only the little picture of the moment, there is a good chance our mind will identify such actions. That is one of the advantages of a well-developed mind. We also can consult with others. It is worth noting that we cannot be absolutely sure the new thing will be better than the old thing. However, experience has shown us that the old thing, the thing we do out of habit, doesn't work, or at least doesn't work in certain circumstances. Thus, while we can only hope that our new thing will work, or at least work better, we know for sure the old thing doesn't work or doesn't work very well.

Once we have identified new possible actions, we can then choose to do one of them. Importantly, it is from our spiritual center that such *choices* are best made. It is also from our spiritual center that we most strongly sense control of our hands, arms, feet, and mouth.

Habits are said to "fit like a glove" which is just another way of saying they feel right. Thus, whatever new behavior we do, it will not have that quality of "fitting like a glove." Instead, it will most likely feel odd, weird, and strange and "not like me." Nothing is wrong! As we have already seen, that is just what happens when anyone acts contrary to a way of acting that is done quickly and easily and without much awareness. Those feelings of strangeness are just part of the habit change process.

Additionally, when we begin acting differently, our performance will not be nearly as good as it might eventually become. Quite often we begin awkwardly and ineptly even if later we might perform well and with ease. Once again, nothing is wrong! That is simply part of the process of changing from an old, well-practiced habit to a different behavior.

The important thing to recognize is that if we refuse to experience either "this is odd, weird, and strange and not like me" or performing poorly and awkwardly, at least in the beginning, then it will be impossible to actually change our habit. Why? Because those are exactly the experiences that come when we try to change from our old way of acting to a new one.

One might say these experiences are part of "the price of admission" to acting differently than we have quickly and easily acted up until now. It is part of the price of admission in the same way that raising our awareness was also part of the price of admission to changing something we previously were hardly aware of doing at the time we were doing it. And it is from our spiritual center, rather than from our mind or body, that we are best able to notice and choose. It is also from the spiritual aspect of our being that we can undertake the process of habit chance willingly rather than grudgingly, a fact that further underlines the spiritual aspect of the habit change process.

Evidence shows that it takes between twelve and fifteen months to establish a new habit. The longer we practice this new way of responding, the more we lose the sense that, "this *is not* like me," and build a sense that, "this *is* like me." Additionally, with practice, we tend to lose our awkwardness and our actions are more smoothly performed. In other words, the new behavior becomes more habitual. Even so, we never really get rid of old habits. Once we learn to do something, we still know how to do it and that old way of acting is always around even if its strength lessens as the strength of the new way of acting grows. Another way to make this point is to say that while we can continue adding to our life history, we can't just "throw away" what we already know and return to a time when we didn't know it.

**Urges**

Changing habits often means dealing with urges. If we keep raising our awareness, we likely will begin to notice an "urge" to act before we actually begin acting. We now have the opportunity to do the new behavior before we have started the old one.
We are finally, so to speak, "ahead of the curve." We "see it coming." Though with urges, it is more like we feel it coming. It would be nice if we only had urges to act in ways that worked best for us and never had urges to act in ways that, no matter how well they work in the moment, don't work in the Big Picture we have chosen for our life. Unfortunately, and far more frequently than we would like, we are going to experience urges to act shortsightedly; in ways that work in the moment but not in our life!

We can reduce the frequency and intensity of some urges by controlling the world around us. Bringing cookies home makes it much more likely that we will have urges to eat cookies than leaving the cookies at the store. And, the trouble with temptation is that it is tempting! The thing is, the more we practice giving in to an urge, the better we get at giving in and, on average, the more frequently and more intensely the urge appears. Alternatively, the more we practice resisting an urge, the better we get at resisting and, on average, the less frequently and less intensely the urge appears. The words "on average" are important because sometimes, even when we have been resisting an urge for quite a while, it may suddenly and surprisingly become more frequent and more intense, at least for a short time. Unfortunately, once we give in, the urge again appears more often and with greater intensity even if we had previously resisted for several weeks, months or years. Thus, if you want to reduce frequency and intensity of particular urges, the most effective strategy is to not give in to them.

Raising our awareness as the first step in changing the way we handle urges means becoming more, not less, aware of our urges. From our spiritual center we not only can experience our urges while acting in service of the Big Picture we have chosen for our life even as the urge pushes us to act differently, we also can experience urges willingly. This remains true even as we wish we could act in a new, more effective, way without experiencing urges to act in the old, ineffective way.

Willingly experiencing an urge works better than experiencing it unwillingly. It also works better than trying to fight the urge. Fighting our own urges is self-defeating because we are on both sides. Our body and mind are aspects of our own being, not aspects of someone else. The most effective response is not to fight harder with our self but to contact the fight from our spiritual center and "lay down the weapons" so to speak. It is from the spiritual aspect of our being that we can willingly experience an urge and doing so allows us to learn some important things about urges in general, and our current urge in particular.

Perhaps the most important thing we can learn is that "having an urge" does not equal "acting on the urge." We, in fact, can learn that just because we have an urge to act, even a very, very strong urge to act, when we contact the urge from our spiritual center, we don't have to do what the urge is pushing us to do. From our spiritual center, urges can be experienced as something "we have" rather than something "we are" and as something we can choose to act on or not. Or, said slightly differently, we are our urges and MORE. That MORE includes the spiritual ability to willing choose to act on urges or not. The more deeply we contact this reality, the less fearful we become of urges because the knowledge gained from our repeated spiritual action shows us that no matter the strength of any urge, we can still pick what we do with our hands, arms, feet, and mouth. We cannot learn that we don't have to act on urges we will later regret having acted on if we spend all our time trying not to have those urges in the first place.

A second important thing we can learn from the spiritual move of willingly experiencing urges is that they are a bit like waves – they rise and fall, they come and go. Oddly enough, urges actually seem to hang around longer the more we put effort into not having them exist in the first place.

Spiritual development is about acting *with* thoughts, images, and bodily sensations, including urges, held gently rather than knocking them out of existence and then acting without them. Thus, though there are many actions we cannot do without experiencing certain thoughts and feelings, including the ones we call "urges," those same actions can be taken while willingly holding those thoughts and feelings gently. Spiritual development occurs as we more and more act from our spiritual center and *with* our mind and body rather than by trying to first throw our mind and body away. And the habit of developing spiritually is a habit one can choose to build and maintain.

# Chapter 11
## Fear, Anger, Inaction &
## the Flight-Fight-Freeze Response

Like most creatures, we humans have built-in responses to help us stay alive and make more like us. One of the most important is our flight-fight-freeze response. Lots of people forget about the last possibility. However, sometimes, if we are very still, danger will pass us by. Many English speakers will be familiar with the phrase, "frozen in fear," which reminds us of the last possible response in this three-possibility response system. "Adrenaline" is the name for the main chemical associated with alarm systems of many living beings. When adrenaline is present, we commonly get a number of noticeable bodily sensations including, but not limited to, our heart beating faster and more strongly, our mouth getting dry, as well as our hands or other body parts sweating. This flight-fight-freeze response system, which we might also call our "alarm system," is tightly tied to the Rule of Life, live long enough to make more like me/us, and adaptive for around two seconds to eight minutes. Normally, whatever the outcome, it has happened within this time period. Either the bear killed you, passed by you, you escaped, or you fought it off. Either the tree fell on you, missed you or you got out of the way. Either the car crashed, or it didn't. It just doesn't take that long before "it's over."

Not only can this alarm system help keep you alive when danger is present, it also gets you "ready for action" when you sense possible danger. Exactly which of the three alternatives responses will come first when a sense danger is present may not be clear, but you are activated to do at least one. Maybe, it turns out that you first freeze, and if discovered, you fight, and then flee. Maybe you just flee. The point is, your alarm system not only helps you when danger is right here right now, it helps you be ready for danger that might be "right around the corner" as well.

No living system is perfect, and neither is our alarm system. It would be great if our alarm system never went off when there was no danger and always went off when there was. However, it's faulty. In theory, it can go wrong in two different ways. Either it goes off when there is no danger, or it fails to go off when there is. It is difficult for any being to stay alive long enough to make more like them if that being has an alarm system that fails to go off when danger is present. As the saying goes, "it is better to miss lunch than to be lunch." It is better to have an alarm system that goes off when no danger is present and you miss out on certain possibilities, than to have an alarm system that fails to go off and leaves you dead or seriously injured. Thus, we should learn not to be surprised when our alarm system goes off and there's "nothing there." It may be a mistake, but it's "a mistake we can live with!"

It has been suggested that we distinguish fear from anxiety in the following way. Fear is what you feel when you are out in the forest and encounter a bear that might kill you. Anxiety is what you feel when you are at home having thoughts and images about encountering a bear in the forest that might kill you. The thing is, what we are calling fear and what we are calling anxiety are each working off the same flight-fight-freeze system. Not only can we human beings have our alarm system mistakenly activated when no danger is actually present, as is the case with other living organisms, we can also have our alarm system activated by thoughts and images *about* whatever we respond to as dangerous even when we are in a place where the things we are thinking *about* are far away in time and space. We can try to use words like anxiety and fear to differentiate between the times our alarm system is activated by actual danger rather than thoughts or images of danger, but, from the inside out, it is all the same because it is the same alarm system being activated in both cases. You feel the same fear feelings when you hear a scary story or see a scary movie as you feel when you are where harm might, in fact, happen. This extends to becoming ready for action. Thoughts and images *about* danger can activate your alarm system making you ready for action just as surely as actually being in places where dangerous things might truly happen.

In this way, life is different for human beings than for other beings. Other beings also have alarm systems. And just like our alarm system, their alarm system might go off when no danger is present because, just as for human beings, it is better for all beings to miss lunch rather than be lunch. However, we human beings also have human minds, which means our alarm system not only can be activated by actual or potential danger but also by thoughts and images *about* actual or potential danger. As far as we know, other beings don't have alarm systems that go off when they hear scary stories or think scary thoughts. We do. Just try telling a scary story to chickens, goats or a family pet and see what happens.

Further, because we can experience thoughts or images about danger any time of the day or night, an alarm system that works well for a few seconds or a few minutes can be activated for hours, days, weeks, and even longer. Thus, our fear, anger, and sense of "feeling frozen" can go on and on and on. While there are many advantages to having a human mind, this capacity for our alarm system to remain activated for long periods of time by thoughts and images *about* danger isn't one of them.

Our human mind also can play a rather nasty trick on us. We can have thoughts like, "My bodily sensations are dangerous." Even though this kind of thinking can happen with any bodily sensations, for example sexual sensations, it often happens with the fear sensations. Thus, we may think, "my fear sensations are dangerous," which activates our alarm system, and we then feel the feelings that come with activation. We then respond to those feelings as if the feelings were, indeed, dangerous and we become even more ready for action to deal with the danger – namely the danger of our own feelings. We find ourselves thinking thoughts about our fear sensations like, "It might get worse," and, sure enough, it gets worse.

And it can get even trickier because we also can have thoughts like, "that dangerous thing of feeling fear sensations *might* happen," and our body will become ready for action in response to that thought. "Ready for action" activates the very sensations that we are to be "on the lookout for." Thus, the action of becoming ready for "the danger of our bodily sensations" brings on the very sensations that we are responding to as dangerous, and we easily find ourselves in a vicious cycle of becoming more and more fearful of our own fearfulness.

Similarly, we may not only have thoughts that our bodily sensations are dangerous. We also can have thoughts that our thoughts or images are dangerous. Thus, we may not only relate to our bodily sensations as dangerous, and find that by doing so we have activated, or further activated, our alarm system, we also may relate to our thoughts and images as dangerous and respond as if our thoughts and images were something from which to flee, fight or freeze. In addition to, "don't feel that feeling," we add, "don't think that thought" and "don't image that image!" The result is similar to becoming more and more fearful of our own fearfulness. The more

59

we are trying to fight, freeze or flee from our own thoughts and images, the more we become like a dog chasing its tail. Where can you go to escape your own thoughts, images, or bodily sensations except, possibly, to non-consciousness? A move that is, unfortunately, all too common.

We might not like these aspects of human life, just as we might not like any number of facts about life as a human being. If the word "wrong" simply means, "we don't like it," then many things are wrong in life. But if "wrong" means, "is not part of our nature," then nothing is wrong at all. The *potential* to run our selves around in circles with the way our thoughts, images and bodily sensations can sometimes function is simply part of being human!

Instead of arguing with life as we find it, we can act from our spiritual center and apply the Formula for Serenity in Action. We can willingly acknowledge, accept, give our permission if not our approval, and willingly experience life as we find it. That includes life with our human mind, and its thoughts and images, as well as our human body, which provides a large number of bodily sensations and has an alarm system that works imperfectly.

# Chapter 12
## Mental versus Spiritual Moves
## with Thoughts, Images & Sensations

Our spiritual center provides spiritual response options to an alarm system that can be activated by thoughts and images as well as by actual danger. That's because it is from our spiritual place-from-which that we can notice and choose. Here is how that ability can help us.

Consider the risk of riding in an automobile or an animal-drawn cart. In either case there could be a wreck and we could be killed or injured. Thus, whenever any of us gets into such a vehicle we are taking a risk. As a little experiment, make yourself have this thought, "When I get in the vehicle, there is some risk of being killed or injured." You can say that thought is true in the sense that when you do get in the vehicle there truly is some risk of being killed or injured no matter how small that risk may be. However, from your spiritual center you can also notice that your thought *about* the risk is not, itself, the risk. You can notice that your thought, whether true or not, is a thought – a thought *about* a risk and not the risk itself. You put yourself in contact with the risk by actually being in the vehicle, not by *thinking* about being in the vehicle. And you can apply the spiritual ability of noticing to both actions. You can notice you are *thinking* about a risk when that is what you are doing, and you can notice you are actually taking a risk when that is what you are doing. You also can notice that these are two different things rather than the same thing. Taking a risk can be dangerous. Thinking about one isn't dangerous no matter how frightening it feels. Noticing the difference can help you take the most effective actions for the situation you are actually dealing with.

I want to emphasize that I am talking about the spiritual ability of noticing, in this case noticing thoughts. I am not talking about the mental ability of thinking more thoughts such as, "I can notice that my thought is just a thought." Indeed, you could use your mind and think, "I can notice that my thought is just a thought." That would be the *mental* action of thinking, not the spiritual action of noticing. I am intending that my writing will direct you to distinguish the action of noticing from the action of thinking, including thinking *about* noticing.

Consider it this way. Bodily sensations are silent, and you silently notice them. However, thoughts are not silent. Thus, when you notice thoughts, you notice something that isn't silent. However, the noticing itself is silent, just as it was silent when you noticed bodily sensations. In short, if you are "hearing something," the thing "being heard" is not you doing the spiritual action of noticing because that action has no sound. Noticing is silent even if what is being noticed isn't. Said slightly differently, I am not asking you to employ your mind, an aspect of your being which can produce either thoughts, or sound filled images. I am asking you to employ your spirit, a place from which you can notice without making any sound.

This spiritual ability to notice is useful because the thoughts you think *about* things that are, indeed, dangerous are not the dangerous things your thoughts are about. Similarly, your mental images *of* dangerous things are not the dangerous things the images are of. Vehicular wrecks that can kill you are, indeed, vehicular wrecks that can kill you. Thoughts or images *about* vehicular wrecks that can kill you can be noticed to be only thoughts and images. Trying to fix those thoughts or images can't make you any safer because the thoughts and images are not the danger the thoughts or images are about. Thus, you don't have to spend your time addressing a danger that isn't actually present. You can, instead, spend that time on things that, for you, are more worthwhile.

Just as your thoughts or images of danger can be recognized as only thoughts and images, the bodily sensations you experience with the activation of your alarm system also can be noticed as only bodily sensations. You experience fear feelings because your alarm system has been activated. Like all other beings with alarm systems, it might be activated when there is actual danger, or it might go off when there is no danger – the system doesn't work perfectly. Because you are a human being, it also might be activated by your thoughts or images *about* danger. It might even be activated by the thought that the feelings you experience with the activation of your alarm system are, themselves, dangerous. For example, thoughts such as, "It is dangerous for me to feel the feelings I am feeling" or "These feelings are dangerous to me."

However, regardless of what activated your alarm system and the bodily sensations you experience when it is activated, the feelings, themselves, can be noticed as nothing more, and nothing less, than bodily sensations since, indeed, that is precisely what they are. After all, the experience of your alarm system going off is not whatever it is that set the system off in the first place. That is true whether the thing setting off your alarm system is actual danger, your thoughts of danger, or just a false alarm. No matter the strength or power of your alarm system sensations, you also can notice them from your spiritual center as simply strong, powerful bodily sensations. Why are you able to do this? Because you are more than your bodily sensations or thoughts about them! There is a spiritual aspect to your being in addition to your mind and body. You have a place-from-which to notice thoughts, images, and feelings. A place that is different from them and with which you become a body, a mind, and more.

The spiritual move of noticing that thoughts about things, or images of things, are not the things the thoughts or images are about can help you live more effectively with thoughts and images of dangerous things because you no longer have to get rid of thoughts and images to pursue what you choose to make important in your life. The same can be said when it comes to noticing bodily sensations.

Let me again underline, "noticing" is different from "having thoughts" even if the thoughts are about noticing such as, "I will notice my bodily sensations as only bodily sensations." Noticing is a silent, spiritual move while having thoughts is a mental move, just as creating images is a mental move.

Human beings often try mental moves when their alarm system goes off. For example, a person might think, or at least try to think, "Everything will turn out fine," or "The danger is not very likely to happen, so I'll take the risk," or "If the bad thing happens, I wouldn't like it, but it won't be THAT bad," or even, "To hell with the consequences, I'm doing it any way!" The point is not whether such moves are true or false, or right or wrong or even helpful or unhelpful.

At one time or another I have used every one of these and, likely, you have as well. Taking such thoughts seriously may have been helpful ways of addressing feelings and may continue to be. The point is they are all mental moves to address bodily sensations. Thoughts are not the silent spiritual move of noticing. In this case, the silent spiritual move of noticing that feelings, such as those produced by our alarm system, can be treated as nothing more, and nothing less, than bodily sensations. While noticing feelings simply as feelings, we can employ yet another equally silent spiritual move - *willingly choosing* to move our hands, arms, feet, and mouth in the service of the Big Picture we have willingly chosen for our life. From our spiritual center we can notice and choose regardless of whether our feelings gain strength, loose strength, or stay the same. Said slightly differently, mentally giving yourself instructions to make spiritual moves might help you make those spiritual moves. Even so, the mental move of telling yourself what to do is not the spiritual move that you are mentally instructing yourself to make. Telling yourself what to do isn't doing it even if you tell yourself fifty times! Maybe the mental instructions help you make the spiritual move and maybe they don't. The point is that giving yourself instructions to make spiritual moves when strong bodily sensations are present is a mental, rather than a spiritual, response.

Just as mental moves are not spiritual moves, they also are not physical moves. When I was a college student, I *thought about* studying over and over and over, but often I didn't actually study! My mental move wasn't the physical move of sitting down with the books and trying to get information out of them by taking notes and then reviewing the notes. I often acted as if "knowing *what* to do" was going to be as effective as actually doing it! Similarly, "knowing how to make spiritual moves" is not making them. Instructing yourself to make spiritual moves isn't making them even if mentally giving yourself such instructions to take spiritual action helps you take such action. Just as getting my studying done required actually studying and not the mental action of telling myself over and over, "You'd better get down to studying," noticing strong feelings as nothing more, and nothing less, than strong feelings requires spiritual, not mental, action. The advantage gained by recognizing this distinction, especially when experiencing strong bodily sensations, is that you can act more effectively in the pursuit of your deepest desires instead of finding yourself constantly stuck going round and round your mental racetrack. Most especially, the spiritual move of noticing strong bodily sensations as nothing more, or less, than strong feelings helps you more effectively apply the Formula for Human Liberation: *By willingly doing something unpleasant, and willingly refusing to do something pleasant, in the service of something I willingly choose to make more important, I never have to be a slave to circumstance,* and the Formula for Serenity in Action: *Let me willingly acknowledge life as I find it (as life is, was or may be) even though I may not approve of what I find, have wisdom to see what would be good to change, willingly choose to start, willingly choose to follow through, and be grateful for the opportunity to try to live my life as best I can.*

When it comes to making a spiritual move in relation to our thoughts, we can notice that thoughts are thoughts regardless of the content of those thoughts. If we were working on our *mental* development, we could work to train ourselves to think one set of thoughts rather than another.

If we were working on *spiritual* development, we could work to train ourselves to both *notice* that, no matter what thoughts we are thinking, those thoughts can be regarded as nothing more, and nothing less, than thoughts, and at the very same time, we can choose to act in the service of Big Picture we have chosen for our life - the specific directions and the specific ways of moving in any direction that we have picked for ourselves.

We can say the same thing about images. We could try to make mental images of the outcomes we want rather than images of outcomes we don't want. As before, such moves are not, necessarily, wrong, bad, or mistaken. Perhaps they turn out to prove useful. And just as before, we still would be making *mental* moves rather than *spiritual* ones. With the spiritual aspect of our being we can *notice* that, no matter what images we experience, we can relate to those images simply as the images they are. Rather than work to train ourselves to have this image rather than that image, we could train ourselves to notice that our images can be treated as only images, while at the same time, we also act in the service of the Big Picture we have chosen for our life. As before, the first moves work on *mental* development while the second work on *spiritual* development.

Sometimes individuals will try to directly control their bodily sensations with activities, for example long periods of exercise, or with substances rather than with thoughts or images. These kinds of moves are more "physical" than mental. Nevertheless, these physical moves are included here because they help differentiate spiritual development from other kinds of development. The distinction is similar to the distinction described above. Rather than trying to change or fix one or more bodily sensations, the aim of spiritual development is to notice bodily sensations as nothing more, or less, than bodily sensations while acting in the service of the Big Picture you have chosen to make your life about.

Could you "do something" or "take something?" Perhaps you could and there is not, necessarily, anything bad or wrong about doing so. There is nothing wrong or bad about getting cancer treatment if you have cancer or taking a headache pill if you have a headache. The point is that such moves would not be the kind of spiritual move being described here. Trying to control feelings is not the spiritual move of not being controlled by them through noticing that, however, powerful, they are nothing more, or less, than feelings.

I have given a lot of talks over the years and, once the group I am speaking to gets large enough, there is a very good chance my alarm system will go off. My heart will pump fast enough and hard enough that I become aware of it when, typically, I would not notice. My mouth gets a little dry. It's hard to focus on the words I planned to say, even if I printed them out ahead of time and they are right in front of me. I feel kind of "jumpy" or "edgy."

Typically, I take some steps in preparation for this possibility. I print out what I intend to say in very large type so that even when I am having trouble focusing on the words I want to say, I can still see them well enough on the page. I also make sure I have some water close at hand. These physical moves help me give my best talk, even as I experience my alarm response in contrast to either being controlled by my fear feelings, or skip giving my talk at all to avoid feeling them. However, these physical moves are not so clearly focused on noticing my alarm response sensations as nothing more, and nothing less, than alarm response sensations.

Developing and using our mind and body are good things. Our mind and body are neither inferior to our spirt nor enemies of it. They are simply different from it. Developing spiritually allows us to notice thoughts, images, and feelings without becoming bullied by, or overly entangled, with them because we experience our self as more than mind and body. We have a place-from-which we can notice and choose no matter what our thoughts are telling us, our images showing us, or what our body pushes for. Each time we act from our spiritual center, we develop that place from which we can willingly serve the Big Picture we have chosen for our life even when our thoughts, images and feelings make it seem that we can't.

# Chapter 13
## Fear: Escape, Avoid, or Encounter

If you go to the berry patch, a dragon might come. You can avoid the dragon by avoiding the berry patch, but you won't have any berries. In order to have berries, you have to go to the berry patch and risk contact with the dragon. If you don't take the risk, you don't get the berries.

In this little metaphor, the berries are life lived serving the Big Picture you have chosen for your life. The dragon is composed of 1) the risk of getting what you don't want, 2) the risk of failing to get what you do want and 3) the sorrow that comes if either, or both, of these happen. In short, the dragon is the risk of sorrow. Life will allow you to avoid or escape situations where you risk sorrow. It won't stop you. However, when you continually avoid or escape the risk of sorrow, you can't serve the Big Picture you have chosen for your life. Perhaps you will survive, but you can't thrive. Pursing whatever you most deeply desire cannot be done without risking sorrow.

**The Moment of Encounter**

A few pages back, you were asked to experiment with the thought, "When I get in the vehicle, there is some risk of being killed or injured." and you had an opportunity to notice that the thought about the risk is not, itself, the risk. Rather, the thought can be contacted as nothing more and nothing less than a thought. So, what happens when you get in the vehicle and actually take the risk?

We can add that, in this case, you are *knowingly* taking the risk. When you take a risk, and don't know it, you have a different experience than when you knowingly take a risk. If you are old enough, you will be able to look back on your life and recall times when you took risks but simply didn't know it. In those times your alarm system did not activate because in those times you had no sense of danger.

So, what happens when you knowingly take a risk? The answer is you feel the risk – your alarm system makes you "ready for action." That is, you feel the literal bodily sensations that come with activation of your alarm system. Nothing is "wrong." Whether you call the feeling "fear," "anxiety," "stress," or any other name, you are simply experiencing what it is like to feel a risk you are knowingly taking.

It has been said that courage is not the absence of fear. Courage is making something more important than being afraid. Raising your "Courage Quotient" is right in line with spiritual development because it is the practice of making your Leading Principles and values more important than thoughts, images, and bodily sensations, especially fear sensations. Willingly experiencing, rather than avoiding, these thoughts, images and feelings that so regularly show up when you attempt to follow your Leading Principles and act consistently with your values is not some trick for getting rid of them. Rather, it is the practice of making something more important, namely acting from that place-from-which you can willingly choose to follow your Leading Principles and willingly act according to your values even as you also experience certain thoughts and feelings while doing so. This kind of courage is running your life from the spiritual aspect of your being rather than from the bodily or mental aspect. Seeing how high you can raise your Courage Quotient is a lifelong part of the kind of spiritual development outlined here.

Perhaps there are things you can do to reduce the risk you are taking when you get in a vehicle. If you are driving, and the vehicle is an automobile, you can put both hands on the steering wheel. You can watch the road, not the birds flying near the road. You can pay attention to the signs that are often put up along the road. Those signs are there to help drivers drive more effectively. Buckling your seatbelt may reduce your risk of harm if you are in a wreck, but it won't reduce your risk of being in one!

These are all things you can do to drive more effectively and by driving more effectively, you reduce risk. These actions are done by focusing on actual driving in contrast to focusing on thoughts or images about the risk you are taking or focusing on the feelings that come with knowingly taking that risk. You make something more important than those thoughts, images, and feelings. Metaphorically speaking, you are putting your "eyes on the prize." In this case, the "prize" is driving effectively. You have control over how you use your ability to notice. And, you can develop the ability to pick what you make important even as you are invited by life circumstances to place your focus elsewhere. Picking where you put your focus, even as you are invited to focus on your thoughts, images and bodily sensations is another spiritual move.

## *Activity 9: Foreground / Background*

*Focus on your right hand for a few moments.*
*Now switch your focus to your left foot for a few moments.*
*Now back to your right hand for a few moments.*
*And back to your left foot for a few moments.*
*And back to your right hand for a few moments.*
*And back to your left foot for a few moments.*

Check and see if, for you, it is correct to say that each time you switched your focus, what you were previously focusing on went into the background. It didn't go away. It went into the background. If you had tried to get it out of the background, it would have been in the foreground. Whenever you "put your eyes on the prize" there will very often be something in the background. You will act more effectively by simply leaving it there. If you try to get it out of the background, then, in the moment you switch your focus, whatever was in the background becomes the thing that you are now prizing.

Admittedly, sometimes thoughts, images, or bodily sensations seem to stomp their way into the foreground. They demand that you give them some attention. If you have ever been to a public event where the seating was bleachers, you have a nice metaphor for how to handle this situation. Bleachers are simply rows of a very long flat surface on which individuals can sit. Each row rises high enough above the previous one so that those seated in that row can see over those seated in front of them. The thing about bleachers is that there is often more room for people to sit than there might seem to be. If you have ever been to an event with seating in the form of bleachers, you may have noticed that even though there seems to be little room left for anyone to sit, when the good-looking twins show up, people tend to move closer to each other, and, by doing so, make enough room for this attractive duo to sit down.

I gave the example of the good-looking twins because the ugly fat kid can take up as much room as two people. And, the room is there! We may have thoughts, images, or feelings we consider ugly, and we also have room for them in our metaphorical bleachers. Following the Formula for Serenity in Action, we can hold them gently. If they are the price of admission to taking a risk, we not only can pay, but we can also pay willingly. Rather than fight or argue with those experiences that would have us divert our focus, we can give them a place in our metaphorical bleachers and then return to putting our eyes on the prize – to focusing on what fits with the Big Picture of Leading Principles and values we have chosen for our lives.

Sometimes when I give this example, folks object to my referring to someone who is overweight and physically unattractive. However, in truth, there are overweight and physically unattractive individuals. Many of us have felt like that person even if by some objective standard we weren't that overweight or that physically unattractive. The thing is, whether you were an ugly fat kid or just felt like one, wouldn't it have been nice if folks made some room for you?

Well, you now have the chance to do that for those ugly fat experiences that, no matter how unwanted, belong to no one but you – *your* thoughts, *your* images, *your* bodily sensations. And, from your spiritual center, you are more than only thoughts, images, and feelings. Thus, from your spiritual center you have the option, the potential choice, of acting kindly toward them. You can even do it willingly. You have the option of giving them a place to rest while, from your spiritual center, you turn your focus back to what you most deeply want to make important.

### And If You're a Passenger?

What if you get in the vehicle as a passenger? If you are a passenger, you are not driving the car. You can speak to the driver about the way you would like the vehicle to be driven, but there is nothing you can directly do about reducing risk of being injured except buckling up your seatbelt. Literally, you are not in the right place to reduce other risks because you are not in the driver's seat. Pushing hard on the passenger seat floorboards, or forcefully gripping some part of the car, does not make you safer even if, at that moment, you *feel* safer. For that matter, even if you are the driver, grabbing the steering wheel with more force than is needed to control the wheel doesn't reduce the risk either.

The point is that there are things you can do to reduce risks and things you cannot do. Trying to change your thoughts or images about risks are not effective risk reduction strategies because thoughts and images about risks are not the risks. Trying to change the bodily sensations that occur when your alarm system is activated is typically not an effective risk reduction strategy either. Your alarm system helps you deal with danger. It is not the danger itself.

**The Takeaway**

Hopefully, the words you have just read appeal to your mind. If they were successfully written, they "make sense" and you "understand" what to do. However, what they describe is not more mental activity. The activities to be done are not more talking, more thinking, or more imagining. The activities to be done are noticing and choosing – noticing with discernment and choosing to effectively move your body (your hands, arms, feet, and mouth) consistent with your Leading Principles and values.

The noticing to be done is summed up by the words "my bodily sensations are not the danger." And, that noticing is not thinking more thoughts such as, "my bodily sensations are not the danger" or "time to effectively move my body." The choosing is not thinking thoughts like, "this is *why* I'm acting," or mentally re-minding yourself about the Leading Principles and values that make up the Big Picture you have chosen for your life even if thinking those thoughts help. Choosing is moving your hands, arms, feet, and mouth in the service of that Big Picture, not thinking about your Big Picture, or thinking about serving it. Doing all these things willingly is not thinking about doing them willingly. If mental action helps facilitate spiritual action fine! Just notice that no matter how helpful, mental activity is never spiritual activity even if your mental action helps your spiritual action. Developing the ability to notice the difference between making a mental move and a spiritual move is part of what spiritual development is all about.

# Chapter 14
## Hostile Aggression

In addition to escaping or avoiding when feeling afraid, we may also feel angry and act aggressively – the "fight" part of the flight-fight-freeze response. Again, it is worth noting that our alarm response functions work well over a very short period. With hostile aggression, the danger either is killed or moves away and, fairly quickly, it's over.

All the issues we previously noted are still in play. First, our alarm response may occur when no danger is present, a "mistake we can live with." Thus, we may hostilely and aggressively respond when nothing is there. Second, we may respond to our thoughts and images about danger as if they were the danger and we are angrily aggressive in response to our thoughts and images about danger even though that which the thoughts and images are about is nowhere around. Just as we saw with fleeing, our thoughts and images can turn an alarm response, in this case hostile aggression, that may function well over a short period into a response that extends over hours, days, months and even longer.

### Righteous Indignation
I like to say that righteous indignation is the drug of choice for humans because when you have the sense that you are personally sent by the powers of the universe to TEACH (whoever) A LESSON THEY WILL NEVER FORGET, it can be a pretty big high and, once developed, a hard habit to give up. English speakers will sometimes say they are, "all steamed up" and that, "It feels like I'll blow up if I don't let off the steam." In such moments there is an alternative to "letting off the steam." That alternative is "turning down the flame."

When teaching about fire, instructors often use what is called the "fire triangle" because fire can be seen to be a function of heat, oxygen, and fuel. I'd suggest the fire of righteous indignation has its own triangle that fires people up. That triangle is composed of 1) downgrading someone's personhood, 2) demandingness and 3) entitlement. Here is what I mean by each of these terms.

By downgrading someone's personhood, I mean responding to them as if they were somehow fundamentally less. You respond as if that person is not quite as fully human as you, or other members of your group. It is as if you are a wave on the ocean looking at another wave and insisting that, while you are made of water, it is not. Or, that if it is made of water, the water is inferior to yours. Additionally, we not only become righteously indignant in relation to humans. Just about anything can become the object of our ire. If the object of comparison is not another person but some non-human aspect of existence, then that other aspect of existence also is responded to as "less than me and my group."

By demandingness I mean relating unwillingly, rather than willingly, to your experience of a person, thing, or condition. Rather than accept life as you find it, you behave in that moment as if things simply MUST be different than they, in fact, are. You respond as if the world requires your permission to be as it is, was or may be and you refuse to give that permission.

The last part of the triangle is entitlement. It is possible to make a social agreement with one or more people that if you do something, the other person, or persons, will do something in response. Thus, when we say, "If you will do this, I will do that," and the other person agrees, we have, so to say, "struck a bargain." When the first person completes their part of the bargain, then that person may say something like, "having done my part, I deserve (or I am entitled) for you to do yours." Basically, that's how making a social agreement works. There is a social arrangement whereby each participant is entitled, in the social sense of that word, to receive what has been agreed to if they have kept their part of the bargain.

However, it is also true that people back out. They don't keep their agreements. If it is the kind of agreement that can be taken to a court, and a court is available, one person might take the other to the court. Sometimes there is no opportunity to get into a court. Sometimes, the court does not insist the agreement be kept. Sometimes, even though the court rules the agreement is to be kept, there is no enforcement of that judgment. This is not the kind of entitlement I am talking about when it comes to righteous indignation.

Rather than a sense of social entitlement, I am talking about a sense of what we might call, for lack of a better phrase, "cosmic entitlement." It is as if somehow the universe was supposed to be guaranteeing our social arrangements. Alternatively, we act not so much as if the universe is underwriting our social agreements but as if we could actually make contracts directly with the universe; as if we can get a guarantee from the universe that if we do our part, the universe will do its part. It is a sort of entitlement in capital letters. Just as things MUST go a certain way in the second part of the triangle, a person has the sense that he or she is ENTITLED for them to go that way.

By putting these three together, humans can get themselves pretty steamed up. Let's see.

### Activity 10: Contacting Righteous Indignation

*The purpose of this activity is simply to make contact with how righteous indignation works. If the exercise is effective, the fire will grow big and hot, and you will feel the steam rising. Your job is to notice how righteous indignation works. By itself, all that will happen is that you will "feel the heat." While it is true that you can bring harm to yourself, and other aspects of existence, by what you do with your hands, arms, feet and mouth, this exercise is not about moving your body and, therefore, the exercise is not about harming. Rather, this exercise is about noticing. It is about noticing how the components of righteous indignation work together to "steam you up." Once you better know how the process works, you will have a greater choice over whether you "raise the heat" or choose to "turn it down."*

*Begin by recalling a time someone or something caused you pain, or by forecasting a time when it might happen in the future. If you are feeling pain right now, that also is a good place to start. Consider the place from which your pain comes. Who, or what, failed to give you what you want or gave you what you did not want? Who, or what, brought, or might bring, this sorrow into your life? Once you have identified the source, cultivate the sense, the thought, the belief, the image, the feeling that the source of your pain being less than you: not as good, not as worthy, "less–than" in some fundamental way. Not just taller or shorter than you. Not just larger or smaller than you. Not just different from you. But essentially, fundamentally, importantly LESS than you and the ones you care about.*

*Once you have been able to experience the source of your sorrow as fundamentally less than, begin to add that what has happened, is happening or might happen simply MUST not be allowed. Is it wrong? - perhaps. Is it painful? – surely. And this wrong, this pain simply HAS TO be changed. This wrong CANNOT and MUST NOT be. Notice what it's like to give yourself this sense of refusal and to feel any energy that may come with it. Notice where you feel that energy in your body. Any steam rising? Are the flames of righteous indignation growing? If so, exactly where and how are they manifesting. What thoughts or images or bodily sensations are present? Are they bringing you to a boil or an even stronger boil?*

*Now let's stir in the last ingredient – entitlement. The TRUTH is you DON'T DESERVE this pain. The TRUTH is you are ENTITLED to something different. It's so unfair! You DON'T DESERVE this to happen to you! You DESERVE better! It's only RIGHT that you be treated differently than the painful way life has gone or might go. You should not be denied fulfillment of your deepest desires, hopes and dreams. A just world calls for something else and you, and those you care about, DESERVE justice!*

*Now that you have an experiential sense of each component, let them mix with one another. Let each reinforce each other. Immerse yourself in the sense of fundamental superiority to the source, or potential source of your pain. What do you notice? What is happening in your body? Exactly where in your body is it happening? What are the thoughts that arrive? What are the images? Are they moving pictures or still pictures? Are they moving pictures with sound? Check out any ability you may have to make the flames grow or turn them down. For at least a moment, fully give yourself to the experience, of being DEEPLY and FULLY RIGHTEOUSLY INDIGNANT so you can more completely know it. If useful, go through the descriptions above again. Is the experience powerful? Is it frightening? Is it exhilarating? Is it threatening? Whatever it is, allow yourself to know each aspect and become familiar with it. This is your chance to directly experience righteous indignation and know it more intimately, your chance to know it as it is, for what it is. What more can you learn? You might find that attempting to study the experience changes it. If so, occasionally, take a moment to fully step into the full fury of the experience in order to know each aspect and the combination more clearly.*

*After you have a sense of what giving yourself to righteous indignation is like, see what it is like to let the flames die down. The thought of their less-than-ness, can you notice it as a thought? Are you required to take that thought so seriously, or could you willing*

*make a different choice? If you notice you could willingly make
another choice, then willingly choose to hold the thought lightly – as
just one of many possible thoughts. Now try doing the same with
demandingness. "They HAVE TO," "It MUST," and so on. Try
sensing those thoughts as only sounds in your head – as only words
you connect to lightly and then even more lightly. Ask yourself, "Do
I have a choice to willingly hold on to these words tightly or
loosely?" If I find that I have a choice, what is it like to tighten my
grip? What is it like to loosen it? What is it like to just let go?*

*Similarly for entitlement. Words – again. Pictures – again.
Feelings – again. Can I willing make a choice about my relationship
with the words and pictures and feelings of entitlement and
deservingness? What is it like to be in a tight, solid, locked-in
relationship with the thoughts, images, and feelings of entitlement?
What is it like to be in a loose, light, gentle relationship with the
thoughts, images, and feelings of entitlement? If the flames are going
down, do I miss the heat and energy? Do I miss the sense of power?
Am I relieved? What is this experience like? Where is it in my body –
exactly where – exactly what are these feelings like?*

If the previous activity was successful, you have noticed the
role those certain thoughts, images, and bodily sensations can play as
flames of righteous indignation rise and fall. The more seriously you
treat them, the more you get "steamed up" even to the point that you
feel like "exploding." Alternatively, if you notice thoughts simply as
thoughts, images simply as images or feelings simply as feelings,
their power diminishes. This noticing is a spiritual move that, once
again, can be contrasted with mental moves such as generating more
thoughts to prove that the first set of thoughts are wrong, incorrect,
or not true.

For my own part, I would happily agree that we are all equally
members of the same human family and the same universe rather
than some of us are special while others are not. I would happily
agree that the world does not HAVE TO go the way I claim it has to
because if it really did HAVE TO go that way, it already would be
going that way and we wouldn't be having a conversation about it! I
also would happily agree that none of us has a "note from the
cosmos" entitling us to life going this way rather than that way.
Check your pockets. Where's the note? While I might agree with all

these mental moves, the point is that is exactly what they would be – mental moves, rather than spiritual ones.

There is nothing wrong with using your mind to sort out right versus wrong, or truth versus error, or any other dichotomy regarding thoughts. Such activity can be quite useful at times. The point is that engaging in such activity may help you develop mentally, but it isn't an activity that helps you develop spiritually. While the spiritual aspect of your being allows you to pick what you do with your hands, arms, feet and mouth regardless of your thoughts, images and bodily sensations, it also allows you to notice your thoughts, images and bodily sensations as simply thoughts, images and feelings and choose how seriously you take them based on the Leading Principles and values that compose the Big Picture you want your life to be about. If they help, take them seriously. If they don't help, don't take them seriously. Developing your ability to make these spiritual moves is part of growing spiritually. Put this kind of development in the service of your Leading Principles and values and you further extend your spiritual growth. If you haven't picked going through life burning with righteous indignation as a valued way of being in the world, then use your spiritual powers to let the flames die down as you pursue the Leading Principles and values that you have picked.

**Insistent versus Indignant**

Fighting is one part of our alarm response which, when it functions well, keeps us, and those we care about, alive and unharmed. The thing is, how often do you really find your life, or the lives of your loved ones, at risk in a way that fighting will save you or them? Most individuals reading this material just don't have that many encounters with lions, tigers, bears, wolves, or anything else that we have to fight off. Most of us are not literally in a kill-or-be-killed war zone battling with other humans even if it feels like we are. However, we do have many places in our lives where being insistent or persistent pays off and there is a big and important difference between righteous indignation on the one hand and deep desire, grit, determination, or stick-to-itiveness on the other.

If you have ever dug a hole, you know that one or two shovels full of dirt doesn't get the job done. You have to persist. However, you don't have to persist angrily or hostilely. You don't have to fight the dirt out of the hole. Persisting, alone, will get the job done. Being insistent with yourself about persistently acting in the service of your chosen Leading Principles and values even when you don't feel like doing so is an important part of developing spiritually. And you need not be righteously indignant with yourself, or anyone else, to do that. There is a difference between a firm hand and being shoved, pushed, or punched. A firm hand may be important to your success. Alternatively, how often have shoving, pushing, and punching proved to be that helpful? Letting go of righteous indignation isn't about giving up and letting the world walk all over you or those you care about. On the contrary, it is about refusing to let the fight part of your flight-fight- freeze system sidetrack your spiritual development. You will always have your alarm system. You cannot first get rid of your it and then develop spiritually. The only kind of spiritual development possible is one that takes our alarm system along with it. But taking our alarm system along is not the same as letting it run the show!

# Chapter 15
## Freeze

If we are very still, danger will sometimes pass by. This is the third aspect of our flight-fight-freeze system. It has much more in common with the flight-fear aspect of our alarm system than the fight-anger aspect because it is more about avoidance than engagement. When we "flee," we actively attempt to get away. Similarly, freezing aims to avoid whatever it is we assess to be dangerous. It is often suggested that if attacked by a bear the person should "play dead" and the bear will lose interest. While the wisdom of this move has not always been confirmed, it illustrates that doing nothing rather than something may be the best way to deal with danger. The danger may just go away all on its own. Nevertheless, even though we aren't actively doing anything, our alarm system is still activated. We often can feel our heart pumping, even pounding, as we wait motionless for the danger to pass us by.

If you are following the Leading Principles and values you have chosen for the Big Picture of your life, there are a lot of things you won't be doing. That is mainly because there are a lot of other things you will be doing - things that do serve your Big Picture. And typically, you cannot do things that serve, and fail to serve, at the same time. Though the freeze aspect of your alarm system is urging, don't move, most of the time, movement is exactly what is required to serve your values and Leading Principles. And, of course, while experiencing the urge to "freeze," you may additionally have thoughts like, "don't move," "be still," or "keep quiet."

Spiritual development, as we have seen, isn't about first getting rid of your alarm system and then developing spiritually. It is about acting from your spiritual center even while experiencing the thoughts, images and bodily sensations that come along with an activated alarm system. From your spiritual center, you can willingly acknowledge and willingly choose. You can willingly acknowledge, accept, or give your permission to experience thoughts, images, and bodily sensations as what they are, namely as nothing more and nothing less than thoughts, images, and bodily sensations, and also willingly choose to move your hands, arms, feet, and mouth in ways that fit with the Big Picture you have chosen for your life. As you develop spiritually, you more and more learn that you can act even as you feel frozen and become more skilled in doing so.

However, on very rare occasions, humans, like some other beings, experience what is called "tonic immobility." On these occasions of tonic immobility, you not only feel frozen, but you also actually cannot move. The experience commonly lasts, at most, a very few minutes. If you experience tonic immobility, then do your best to experience it willingly. When movement is in fact an option, as it will soon be, you can notice that sense of feeling frozen and willingly choose movement. Not just any movement, but movement that serves your values and Leading Principles.

Just as we saw before, you could try to get yourself going with mental moves. Thoughts like, "I can do this," "wisdom requires action," "it's only my alarm system," "I'd better get going," and many other thoughts, might indeed help. And, just as before, these are all mental rather than spiritual moves. Minds can be good servants and there is nothing wrong with developing those abilities. However, developing your mind is not developing your spirit. From your spiritual center you can willingly notice and willingly choose.

If you do begin to move, you may notice a subtle, or not so subtle, shift from the freeze mode to the flight mode of your alarm system. Now the push from your body and mind is more toward escape and active avoidance rather than passive immobility. That shift takes us full circle because it was the flight aspect of our alarm system with which we began.

It is less common to shift into the fight mode. However, if that is what happens when you unfreeze, you still retain your ability to act from your spiritual center and serve the Big Picture of the life you have chosen even as you experience righteous indignation and are pushed toward hostile aggression.

Procrastination can be seen as closely associated with freezing. We might say that prioritization is putting off until tomorrow things that are best done tomorrow while procrastination is putting off until tomorrow things that are best done today. Admittedly, the experience of procrastinating seems to slip between freezing and fleeing. Sometimes, when putting off things until tomorrow that are best done today, is best characterized by "stay still and wait." At other times, it seems more like "flee and avoid." It is interesting to again notice how our mind comes into play.

Typically, procrastination is not about failing to act at all. It is about failing to act until the last possible moment. If we start addressing the issue in a timely way, we quickly find ourselves experiencing thoughts, images, and bodily sensations we would rather not experience. Perhaps they are thoughts that our actions *might* fail, and we feel afraid or that they are thoughts that our actions *will* fail, and we feel sad and dejected. By putting off action, we avoid these experiences. We might say that having these thoughts and feelings are the price of admission to taking action, and since we refuse to pay the price, we cannot act.

However, once we sense the deadline to be close enough, we spring into action almost as if the deadline were a charging monster we are trying to escape. The main focus of our action is avoiding the negative experiences of inaction rather than achieving something positive. Thus, procrastination, from start to finish, is more about our alarm system than anything else. At first, we freeze, flee, or actively avoid our thoughts and feelings that come along with, and are the price of admission to, actions aimed at achievement. Later, when we finally do act, our actions are more to avoid the consequences of failing to act than in the service of actively pursuing our values and Leading Principles.

In addition to avoiding action, individuals may worry. Worry is one of those responses that feels like we are addressing an issue when we are not. It seems as if we can travel forward in time, fix the future, and return to the present with a now certain future toward which we can calmly proceed because that future has been fixed. Rumination is the same kind of effort, only we travel backwards in time to fix the past. Unfortunately, both are illusions that we recognize once we return to the present moment and find the past remains whatever it was, and the future remains unknown. If we aren't careful, we can easily become trapped in a repeating cycle of traveling in time to fix something from the past or future only to return to here and now and finding these efforts didn't work. Even so, we find ourselves repeatedly tempted to try again because we feel so firmly that, with one more effort, the fix can be made to work. The cycle is broken by 1) noticing these invitations to go traveling, 2) remaining in the present moment while allowing the invitations to come and go, and 3) willingly acting on our Leading Principles and values.

# Chapter 16
## From "I Can't Believe It" to
## "I Can Begin to Make Peace with It"

Unexpectedly terrible things happen. News reports make clear they happen to others. They also happen to us. Sometimes we had a role in these terrible events. Other times we didn't. Following these experiences, we might find ourselves in that psychologically disorienting place we attempt to express with words like, "I can't come to grips with it!" or "I can't get my head around it!" or "I can't believe it!" Psychologically, it is as if we are listening to a radio with nothing but static.

Contacting the experience over time will allow us to move from "I can't believe it" to "I can believe it." The psychological impact of a few days of day-in-day-out living in the aftermath of a flood, earthquake, tsunami, or mudslide typically moves us from "I can't believe it" to "I can." Only then are we in a position to make peace with what we formerly could not even believe; to willingly acknowledge what we have finally "gotten our head around."

Coming to believe it is different than understanding it. The latter is one way our mind attempts to help. However, there are many things that we do not understand but we readily believe. Spend a few minutes noticing a flat tire and, though you may not understand the why of the tire being flat (nail, screw, sharp rock, piece of glass), you will soon believe that it is, indeed, flat.

Phrases like, "I can't get my head around this!" lead us to respond as if the issue is intellectual, as if our mind, the Commander in Chief of addressing intellectual puzzles, is the best aspect of our being to employ. However, this is not really a figuring-it-out issue. Thus, "trying to understand" is not that helpful. Rather, it is a noticing issue. It is an issue of noticing long enough to allow what is being noticed to move us from "I can't believe it" to "I can."

Noticing is one of our spiritual abilities, but so is willingly acknowledging. Because both noticing and willingly acknowledging take place from the spiritual aspect of our being, it can be tricky to recognize which spiritual move is the more effective one when addressing "I can't believe it." Yes, it is important to willingly acknowledge that one is in the psychological place of "I can't believe it" rather than fighting against the experience. However, willingly acknowledging the experience of "I can't believe it" is not what moves a person from "I can't believe it" to "I can." Noticing, over time, is the key factor to achieving such movement.

While ignorance may be bliss, knowledge is often painful and, sometimes, very painful. We do not typically call something "terrible" simply to indicate that it is powerful. We use "terrible" to mean, "powerfully not what we want" – a source of profound sorrow. By continuing to notice, we pay the price of finally believing it. Quite often that price is heartbreak and the tears, sobs, flowing mucus, and bodily shaking that can go with heartbreak.

More often than we might suspect, life does not give us enough noticing time to move from "I can't believe it" to "I can." Perhaps following a deadly car crash, either we, or the dead body of our loved one, is taken away from the scene too quickly to continue noticing the aftermath. Additionally, the car crash itself may have happened in the blink of an eye. Alternatively, we escape the site of the hurricane, tornado, or earthquake, and are quite glad to have done so. However, our changed location makes it impossible to notice what we are, literally, no longer there to notice, namely the aftermath of the catastrophic event.

We might say that at such times, our mind tries to help us out, but not by trying to help us understand. Instead, it gives us images of the experience we are no longer able to notice because the experience passed too quickly, or we are literally no longer in the right place to notice. Such moments call for a rather sophisticated spiritual response.

We could treat the images our mind offers as nothing more, and nothing less, than images. However, experiencing the images in that way reduces the chances the experience will move us from "I can't believe it" to "I can." That transition requires noticing over time and what is to be noticed is not something that is nothing more, or less, than an image. Rather, for the transition to be made, we typically must treat the images of the events as if the images were the actual events. Rather than only *remembering* the moment, we allow our self to psychologically *relive* it. Why? For the purpose of contacting the experience long enough to make the transition from "I can't believe it" to "I can." Just as a movie has one effect if we respond as if we are witnessing actual events and a different effect if we view it as "just a movie," so too with the images our mind provides us under these circumstances. For our noticing to effectively carry us from "I can't believe it" to "I can," we need to make psychological contact with what seem to be actual events rather than only images of them.

If we allow ourselves to psychologically relive a terrible event, we are going to feel the bodily sensations that commonly show up when our fight-flight-freeze response has been activated. Why? Because, psychologically, the terrible thing is happening right now, and our alarm system is commonly activated in such situations. We are likely to feel fearful, even *very* fearful or have urges to strike out or, alternatively, a sense of being frozen in fear. This happens because, when we connect with images of terrible things as if those images actually were the terrible things, we psychologically travel to there-then, or said slightly differently, the experience psychologically travels to here-now. Rather than connect with the experience from the perspective of "it happened there-then" and which is being remembered from the perspective of here-now, we connect to the experience from the perspective of it is actually happening here-now and, psychologically, relive, rather than remember. We do this for a particular purpose: to make the psychological transition from "I can't believe it" to "I can".

When our journey results in activating our alarm system, as it almost certainly will, there is a spiritual move that can help us best handle these powerful feelings. We can gently hold these emotional reactions, these bodily sensations and the thoughts that may come with them, as we continue to notice the images. Said in other ways, we can experience the feelings and thoughts willingly, we can accept them. Rather than fight against the bodily sensations that result from the activation of our fight-flight-freeze system or try to shut off the images in an attempt to make the feelings or thoughts that come with the feelings go away, we can give our permission for our alarm system to be activated in exactly the way it is being activated and continue noticing images long enough to finally arrive at the sorrowful destination of "I CAN believe it."

There is a story of a woman on a journey who found her way blocked by a wide and powerful river. Working persistently, she constructed a boat that allowed her, with determined effort, to make the dangerous, and consequently frightening, transition from one riverbank to the other. She was proud of the work that allowed her to make the difficult crossing. Even so, the boat, and the work that went into building it, had served their purpose. Thus, once on the other side, she left the boat behind and focused on what was useful for the next part of her journey.

It is the same with intentionally treating images of terrible events as if those images were the actual events for the purpose of crossing from the "I can't believe it" side of the river to the "I can believe it" side. Having crossed over by treating images of events as if those images were the actual events, we leave that practice behind. We stop reliving and start accepting. Having crossed the river to the shore of "I *can* believe it," we now work on *willingly acknowledging* (accepting, giving our permission for) the terrible thing we have come to believe actually did happen. A move that wouldn't have been possible when we were on the "I can't believe it" side of the river.

Now standing on the "I can believe it" side of the river, we aim to willingly remember the terrible event as part of our past instead of reliving it as if it were part of our present. Whether these past events seem more to have happened to us or whether we actively participated in them, we can willingly acknowledge what has happened and willingly contact our memories of that past as if they were pictures in a book of photographs.

Memories can still be painful. If memories bring pain, we can willingly hold that pain gently rather than grudgingly fight with it. While our thoughts and images may invite us to go psychologically traveling to some other place and time, we can now choose to notice these invitations and choose to remain, psychologically speaking, here and now. We can willingly acknowledge these thoughts and images as nothing more, and nothing less, than thoughts and images and allow them to come and go, just as our breath comes and goes, even as we remain here, in this place, and now, in this moment.

Should we ever again find ourselves on the "I can't believe it" side of a river, we can willingly relive the past with the aid of images and hold gently the thoughts and feelings that come with that reliving until we make the transition from "I can't believe it" to "I can."

While forgiveness and reconciliation will be soon and thoroughly covered, it is important to mention them here. When the events we finally have come to believe are sensed to have happened to us, then the potential targets for the spiritual actions of forgiveness and reconciliation will be others and the world in general. However, when the events we have finally come to believe are those in which

85

we have actively participated, then the spiritual actions of self-forgiveness and self-reconciliation will also be required. Without strongly developed capacities to forgive and reconcile with the world, others and ourselves and the discernment for exercising these capacities, spiritual development will be importantly stunted. Since there is no place our self can consciously go without also being there, self-forgiveness and self-reconciliations are foundational to the full flowering of our spiritual development.

# Chapter 17
## Anesthesia

Every moment of life contains the possibility of the sorrow. And in so many life moments, what might happen does happen and sorrow arrives with at least sad feelings and, perhaps, tears coming out of our eyes, cries coming out of our throat, mucus coming out of our nose and our whole body shaking. The approach advocated here has been to willingly pursue our deepest desires and to willingly experience our sorrow instead of trying to purge our self of desire as a way to avoid heartbreak.

However, most individuals do not try to address sorrow by getting rid of all desire. Instead, some try to avoid or, at least reduce, sorrow by living small. Instead of pursuing that which they desire most deeply, they pursue what they desire only a little and, thereby, reduce the risk of being hurt too badly. That also has not been the approach advocated here.

Many more attempt to deal with sorrow by anesthetizing it. The basic approach is not to avoid sorrow but not to feel it. The means to achieve this aim are many, and as technology develops, the methods for anesthetizing oneself are growing all the time. From a cost/benefit point of view, the difficulty with addressing sorrow with anesthesia is the cost of anesthetizing sorrow turns out to be greater than the benefit received. What works in the moment doesn't work in our life.

Consider that psychological place that so many people find – the place in which you feel nothing at all. Yes, that place will work to anesthetize sorrow – you won't feel that pain, but you don't feel anything else either! And, not feeling the pain simply doesn't turn out to be worth feeling nothing at all. Those who know this place also know that about as quickly as we decide to leave, the first thing we feel is sorrow. Yes, for a while we don't feel sorrow because we don't feel anything at all, but not feeling anything at all turns out to be a lousy place from which to live our life. And, as soon as we step out of that place, sorrow is right there again. Better to proceed with life as an exciting adventure while letting sorrow pass through us than go to the place where we feel nothing at all. At least that's the approach offered here!

Righteous Indignation provides another form of anesthesia. While sorrow is deflating, righteous indignation is energizing. While sorrow hurts, with enough righteous indignation we hardly feel the pain at all. That may seem like a lot of upside, but the downside is a life of almost never-ending hostility. That isn't living life as an exciting adventure either and, further, day-in-day-out hostility is as life threating as smoking twenty cigarettes every day!

Alternatively, there are the many substances you can drink, snort, smoke or inject. They, too, anesthetize sorrow. For a few moments you feel "good," or "right," or "whole" or "normal" or anything but the feelings that come with anticipating, or actually experiencing, life's heartbreaks, however large or small those heartbreaks may be. Yes, you do feel that way for a few moments, perhaps even a few hours. But you soon find the anesthesia wears off and you focus more and more on once again deadening the pain instead of living the exciting adventure. The time and treasure spent on anesthesia is time and treasure not spent on what you most deeply care about.

With enough time and treasure spent anesthetizing yourself in one way or another, you may even lose touch with that about which you most deeply care. Life may come to be experienced as not much more than a moment-to-moment pinball machine, in which you bounce first here and then there. It is a life lived only for the moment, but a moment that can hardly be contacted through the fog of anesthesia or the single-minded search for more of it.

Anesthesia can also be accomplished through the distraction of busyness. The main formula is staying so busy doing whatever it is that we don't notice our sorrow. In this form of self-anesthetizing, what we stay busy doing is unimportant. The aim is to stay so focused on the activity that we don't feel the pain of disappointment. And if we do feel that pain, we redouble the intensity of our actions in a desperate effort to insure we won't feel it again. The important part is maintaining our whirlwind of activity lest we feel the very experience our activity is intended to deaden.

Some individuals quite intentionally begin using one anesthesia or another and may even intentionally continue doing so. However, it is just as common, if not more common, that we slip into it. Even if we first began by choosing anesthesia as a way to address the pain of sorrow, we may later lose that intentional or conscious aspect. We find anesthetizing our self has become a habit, something we do quickly and easily and without much awareness. The path of habit change has already been considered: raising awareness until we catch our self in the moment doing the old thing and then begin doing the new one while willingly experiencing both the discomfort of sensing that this new way of acting is odd and weird and strange and "not like me," and the discomfort of performing awkwardly and clumsily rather than with the smooth competence we might eventually develop.

Continually anesthetizing our self can soon stunt our spiritual development because it facilitates the illusion that we can go on an exciting adventure without ever learning to fully experience and willingly acknowledge the sorrow that comes with being fully alive in the world in which we actually live. A world in which we often don't get what we want and often do get what we don't. It is a mistake. And like all mistakes, it is one we don't have to keep making.

# Chapter 18
## Love, Forgiveness, & Reconciliation

From the perspective presented here, love is willingly looking out for someone's, or something's, long-term best interests. You can love a person, a pet, a prairie, or a planet. You can love yourself. Loving from your spiritual center is something you _do_. Something you do with your hands, arms, feet, and mouth rather than, or in addition to, what happens with your thoughts, images, and bodily sensations. And, it is something done willingly. Yes, if you look after someone's, or something's, long-term best interest, you will be looking out after someone's, or something's, long-term best interests, and that is not enough for spiritual love. Spiritual love includes doing it willingly rather than grudgingly. From your spiritual center there is nothing you can do that can't be done - and done willingly.

Thus, you don't have to feel motivated or get your mind straight to love spiritually. This kind of loving is about noticing and choosing. Noticing what counts as acting in someone's or something's long-term best interests and choosing to willingly perform that kind of action. It can be done without affection (i.e., feeling like patting someone on their head or bottom), affiliation (i.e., shared interests) or sexual attraction. It is the kind of loving parents can provide for their teenage offspring when they feel more like hitting them in the head than patting them on the head, no longer seem to have any shared interests, and to whom they are certainly not sexually attracted. You don't have to feel like acting lovingly toward someone, or something, to willingly act lovingly toward that person or thing. It's a choice.

Spiritual loving stands in contrast to what is often called "romantic love." When people are romantically in love, they can truly say to their beloved, "Whatever you want dear," because they don't see that much difference between what they want and what their beloved wants. "It doesn't matter what we do as long as I'm doing it with _you!_" as romantic partners often say. For those romantically in love, being apart seems almost more than they can possibly bear. Such individuals also see their beloved more like a god or goddess than a human being with real human flaws. And typically, those who are romantically in love can hardly keep their hands off each other.

As wonderful as romantic love can be, it doesn't last – especially if the individuals begin maintaining a household together. At some point, one of the individuals realizes, "I don't always want what my beloved wants, I just don't!" Additionally, the veil of near perfection disappears, and the individual realizes that no matter all the good points of their beloved, that person is, in fact, an actual human being with real human flaws. Usually, it isn't too long after one awakens from their romantic dream world that the other awakens as well. Then begins what some have called, "domestic love," which is all about compromise. "We can't have everything we want together because we don't always want the same thing. How much can we have?" It's the same if we "fall in love" with a pet, a house, or a town. The sense of all-upside-and-no-downside eventually disappears, and we are left to address the pet, prairie, plant or whatever as something other than all that we wish it was and once seemed to be.

The kind of spiritual development encouraged here begins with willingly acknowledging the world to be as it is, was or may be. And, that basic aspect of acting from our spiritual center extends to spiritual love as well. Whatever the object of our eventual loving, we first accept, give our permission or willing acknowledge that object to be as it is, was or might be. Then comes the choice of loving, of willingly acting in the long-term best interest of the person or thing we are choosing to love. Willing acknowledgement is a prerequisite for loving because willing acknowledgement is a prerequisite for any spiritual relationship. Thus, loving is something done in addition. That additional something is willingly acting in the long-term best interest the someone or something we aim to spiritually love.

As is so often the case in life, strong minds and strong bodies can be helpful. It is not always a simple matter to sort through the many competing life possibilities to determine what actions really do support the long-term best interests of whomever or whatever we choose to love. Strong minds can be very helpful in making such determinations and certainly more helpful than weak ones. The same thing can be said of strong bodies. Recognizing what to do is one thing. Having the strength and stamina to carry it out can be quite another. Though a strong mind and a strong body can be valuable supports when loving spiritually, it is important they remain servants to our spiritual dimension rather than operating independently of it.

Even if strong is more useful than weak, no mind or body will be infinitely strong which is, in part, why our loving is imperfect. What seems to be in the long-term best interest of the one we intend to love may turn out not to be. And, even if we are correct about what actually serves the long-term best interest of the one, or ones, we seek to love, we may lack the ability to act with sufficient strength or power. Loving as best we can is not loving as best as we can imagine. In the end, our capacities are limited, including our capacity to serve the long-term best interests of anyone or anything.

Love, spiritual or otherwise, is particular. It cannot be aimed everywhere at once. Looking after the long-term best interests of this one, be it a person, pet, prairie, or planet, means you are not, in that moment, looking after the long-term best interests of one, or more, others. Loving one, whomever or whatever that one is, means favoring it, and often favoring it over another. While willing acknowledgement can be done everywhere and all at once, we cannot universally love because what is in the long-term best interest of this one or that one is not in the long-term best interest, or is clearly harmful, of some other one. Eating the seeds of a plant may sustain the life of the organism that eats those seeds and, likely, ensures those seeds won't continue the life cycle of that plant.

This is rarely made clearer than the conflict encountered when loving oneself and loving another. As lovely as it would be if our own long-term best interests and the long-term best interests of everyone and everything else perfectly meshed, they don't. At least some of the time, pursuing our own long-term best interests fails to support, or actively disrupts, the long-term best interests of one or many others and vice versa.

Recall that from the perspective presented here, spiritual development is not about what you pick. It is about that you pick. Spiritual development is not that you love yourself over others or love others over yourself. Spiritual development is about acting from "that place from which." That place from which you can willingly do anything that you can do and taking that action with your mind and body rather than from your mind and body while the spiritual aspect of your being simply comes along for the ride.

Choosing to look after your long-term best interests over the long-term best interests of another, or many others, is not selfish on the view presented here. Selfish is the mental justification that you are entitled to do so. Somehow you are justified, grounded, or warranted in choosing to look after your own long-term best interest. "How dare they block me or even try to block me. Don't they know who I am?! Don't they know I am entitled to care about myself first?!" This is how selfish speaks.

All right! Your mind is giving you some thoughts! How seriously are you taking what your mind is providing? Are you acting from the sense of entitlement your mind provides or are you picking from your spiritual center even as your mind insists on how justified you are in acting this way rather than that?

It is typically the same thing in reverse when your mind tries to fight selfishness. Now they are entitled. Whomever they might be are justified, grounded, or warranted in having you look after their long-term best interests rather than your own. "You *don't* deserve to look out for yourself and certainly not more than you look out for others! Others are entitled to your caring!"

Well, there are some more thoughts! How seriously are you taking what your mind is providing this time? Are you acting from the sense of being un-entitled your mind provides or are you picking from your spiritual center even as your mind insists on how unjustified you are in acting this way rather than that? It can be stunning to realize how many folks do not pursue what they most deeply desire such as a career, a mate or other life choice because their mind tells them, "You don't deserve that!" and never recognize that, from their spiritual center, they have the choice to act no matter what their mind says. Instead, they struggle mightily to convince their mind that they are deserving – a struggle that sometimes lasts all their life. The trick, so to speak, is keeping your mind in the role of advisor, rather than allowing it to have the role of dictator, ruler, or Chief Operating Officer of my Life even as it insists that is exactly the role it should be playing.

**Forgiveness**

I often suggest that forgiveness is just swapping arrogance for willing acknowledgement because it is arrogance when we respond to the world as it is, was or may be with: "But to ME!"

Other people, other beings, or the world in general contact us in ways we do not want or fail to contact us in ways we do want. We even do this to ourselves! Do we willingly acknowledge these facts to be as they are? Often, we do not.

Instead, we hold the facts against someone or something. And, quite often, we don't simply respond with a general sense of outrage, "How dare the world be that way!" but with a quite specific one, "How dare the world be that way TO ME!" As if we were asking, "Doesn't the world know who *I AM*?!" Arrogance prevents us from recognizing the answer: "Just one of the zillions of manifestations of existence." This sense of self-importance is what leads to our asking the question in the first place.

This tendency is why forgiveness becomes essential for our spiritual development. The facts, we might say, are as they are. What we choose to do with the facts is a different matter. We don't have to hold the facts against whomever or whatever. And, if we are already doing so, we can choose to stop. We can choose to forgive.

### *Activity 11: Forgiveness*

*First, write down "the facts," whatever they may be, on a piece of paper. If recounting all the facts takes more than one piece of paper, write the "short version" and let the short version stand for the longer version. Find something hard and relatively flat, a wall will do nicely. Take your index finger and hold the facts against the wall pressing as hard as you can. If you have been holding the facts against another person, imagine the wall is that person and hold the facts against them with all the energy you can muster.*

*If the wall actually was a person, you'd be hurting them. And, the harder you press to hurt them, the more pain you have yourself. Continue imagining the wall was actually a person and notice bringing to pain to another also brings pain to yourself.*

*Quite often in life, no one is actually there for you to hold the facts against. It really is as if you were pushing on a wall. No matter how hard you push, they feel nothing because they are, literally, someplace else. The only pain generated is your own. Notice what it's like when there is actually no one on the other side of your finger to hold the facts against even as you keep on pushing on the wall as hard as you can. Notice what it's like to create your own pain without actually hurting anyone else.*

*Now push lightly on the paper. Notice what it's like to be exerting just enough pressure to keep the facts against the wall.*

*Notice that while the pain goes away, the inconvenience of holding the facts against the wall, or the person the wall represents, remains. Can you pick something up that is more than an arm's length away, let alone go wandering about the world? Try reaching around for things or experiences that are "out of reach" because you keep holding the facts against the wall even as you hold those facts quite lightly. Notice the experience. Is there any sense of being "trapped" or "stuck?"*

*Now, just stop holding the facts against the wall. Simply pull your finger away. The paper falls to the floor. Notice what it's like to just stop pushing, even lightly. Pick up the paper and look carefully at what you wrote. Have the facts changed? No, they have not. Notice what it's like to change your relationship with facts even though the facts, themselves, have not changed. You didn't explain the facts. You didn't excuse the facts. You didn't forget the facts. You didn't understand the facts. You simply stopped holding the facts against something. Notice what it's like to release, to simply stop expending energy in the way you were when you held the facts against the wall. Notice also if your mind objects to you doing something that is so "senseless." Hold the facts against the wall again. Notice what that is like. Release the pressure. Notice what that's like. Repeat this process until you are quite familiar with what it's like to hold the facts against something, or someone, and then release, and to start again and then release again. Would you have to start again? If you did, how much time would have to pass before you released?*

*If you have been holding the facts against yourself, repeat this process while holding the facts against yourself.*

**What Forgiveness Is Not**

Forgiveness is not about excusing, explaining, understanding, forgetting, or changing the facts. It is simply about no longer holding the facts against someone or something. Forgiveness would be unnecessary if you were not already holding the facts against someone, or something. This is why forgiveness is so closely related to willing acknowledgement – giving your permission for the world to be as it is, was or may be. None of us would have use for forgiveness if we were, in this very moment, willingly acknowledging the world as it is, was, or may be. It is our failing to willingly acknowledge in the first place that occasions our need to learn, and practice, forgiving – to learn and practice releasing the facts rather than continuing to hold them against someone or something.

Willing acknowledgment is not approval, and neither is forgiveness. Forgiveness is not about asking yourself to approve of that which you do not approve any more than it is about excusing, explaining, understanding, forgetting, or changing what is, was or may be. The question is, what relationship will you have with what you do not approve? How does it actually work in your life when you hold things you disapprove of, or don't agree with, against something, or someone including yourself? If the answer is, "Great!" then don't stop.

On the other hand, if holding the facts against something or someone, including yourself, isn't working so well, forgiveness is an alternative. Forgiveness is a spiritual move you can make even as your mind insists that making that move doesn't make sense, or your body doesn't feel good about it.

"Holding them accountable! Now that makes sense and certainly will make me feel better!" Blame and condemn. Blame and condemn. Blame and condemn. Might as well stir in a full measure of Righteous Indignation and really get the pot boiling while you're at it!

Consider for a moment the history of blame and condemnation in your own life or the history of the world as far as you know that history. How effective has blame and condemnation ever actually been? Have you really changed when blamed and condemned, including blaming, and condemning yourself? Did you stick with the change once you got far enough away from the one doing the blaming and condemning? Have others quickly come around to your way of doing things when you blamed and condemned them for not having acted that way in the first place? Did they keep it up once you were no longer around? If blaming and condemning were really effective, surely they would have worked by now! Look at how long and how persistently they have been tried!

Whatever it means to you to hold someone, or something, accountable, are you not more able to do it with both hands free as compared to using one of them to hold the facts against that individual who, or circumstance which, you are going to hold accountable? Forgiveness provides you more alternatives to deal with the facts, not less. Forgiveness does this because by allowing facts to simply be facts without you *having to* do a particular thing with them, you are free to do anything with them and to fully participate in whatever choice you make. Yes, you could exercise your opportunity to hold the facts against something, or someone, including yourself. The opportunity to make that move is always there. And once made, you can keep right on making it. However, choosing that option also limits, or eliminates, some of your other options for dealing with those facts. Release the pressure and the facts will remain simply what they are, and you will have both hands free to build the life you are most deeply interested in. The choice is yours. What will you choose to make important?

## A Trick

Perhaps you have noticed a little trick that snuck in during the activity described above. Look at the paper. Does the paper actually contain the facts or just a bunch of words about them?

Often, all that is present right here, right now are thoughts, images, and feelings *about* facts. The facts, themselves, either took place, or are taking place, at some other place and/or time. From our spiritual center we can loosen our grip on, both the facts, and our thoughts, images, and feelings about them when holding tight is not really helping us pursue the Big Picture we have chosen to make our life about. We can make the spiritual move of noticing that our thoughts, images, and bodily sensations can be responded to as nothing more, and nothing less, than thoughts, images, and bodily sensations even as we also keep our eyes on the prize of what we choose to make important with our hands, arms, feet, and mouth right here, right now.

## Reconciliation

Reconciliation is not only giving someone, or something, the opportunity to hurt us again. It is giving them the opportunity to hurt us again in exactly the same way as before. Forgiveness is something we, mainly, do for our self. It removes the pain and inconvenience we experience by holding the facts against something or someone, including ourselves. Reconciliation, typically, involves more than us. As earlier noted, when discussing willingness, reconciliation is not only done with our hands, arms, feet, and mouth. It is also with our heart.

Many will say that reconciliation is about trusting. I suggest it is about risking. We cannot stop knowing what we know and, if we have been hurt, we know it. And once hurt, we realize we could be hurt again. Putting our self in the position to be hurt again is about taking that risk, rather than about trusting that hurt will not happen. No matter how much reassurance is offered about how "it won't happen again," we very well know that it might. Why? Because it already has – at least once! And our mind will point out that what has happened once might happen again. Not only will we find our self being reminded of something that actually happened in the past, we, likely, also will think of new and different ways that we might be hurt in the future.

Reconciliation is choosing to take those risks. And, perhaps not surprisingly, when we knowingly take a risk, we feel the risk. The name of that feeling is "afraid." That fear feeling doesn't mean that something is wrong. Feeling fearful is simply what happens when we are in contact with the reality of knowingly taking a risk.

It is often possible not to reconcile. Just as we can choose to take the risk again with a particular person or a particular circumstance, we can choose not to. Our mind and body can be our servants by providing thoughts, images and sensations related to choosing to take the risk. In the end, however, it is from our spiritual dimension that we can choose anything that we are capable of choosing, including the choice to take, or not take, the risk of reconciliation. It is also from our spiritual center that we can choose to willingly pay the price of admission to knowingly taking a risk including the thoughts and feelings that show up before, during and after the risk taking.

Even so, there are at least a couple of places where reconciliation is not a choice. As long as we are alive, we risk hurting our self, if not in the same way we previously hurt our self, then in some different way. The same is true for the universe of which we are a part. If we are here, we are taking the risk of the world hurting us as it has before or in new and different ways. That is why it is not only important to consider physically reconciling but reconciling with our whole being – with our heart as well as our body.

Look around and you will see many couples that have hurt each other. Even so, they are still living together. They are still sharing a life. By sharing a life, each is, literally, continuing to be in a position to be hurt by the other yet again. We might say that in some couples one, or both, have opened their heart to the possibility of this pain. However, in other couples, one, or both, has closed their heart, so to speak, to the other. They have physically reconciled but they are not reconciled with their whole being.

Just as you could go traveling on an airplane, or on a train, or in an automobile, or in a wagon and, for the whole trip, grip your seat until your knuckles turned white, so also could you take the risk of reconciling but not open your heart to the risk you are taking. You take the risk by getting into and continuing to be in the vehicle just as you take the risk by getting into and continuing to be in the relationship. But you don't take it willingly. One might say that you are only partially taking the risk. You are only taking it physically. You are only taking it with your body but not with your whole being. Your heart, so to say, remains closed. Said another way, you are willing with your feet, but not willing with your heart. Being willing with your heart does not mean being out of contact with the feelings that come with knowingly taking a risk, namely feeling afraid. It means willingly having those feelings while knowingly taking that risk. It is an act of spiritual development that raises your Courage Quotient, your willingness to make something more important than being afraid.

**Partial Reconciliation & Un-forgiveness**
Not only could you reconcile with only your body rather than with your whole being, you also could be unforgiving. Like the member of a couple who continues to live with the person who has hurt them while keeping his, or her, heart closed to that person, you also could continue to live with a person while holding the facts against them. Not only do you keep your heart closed in an effort to protect yourself from future pain, but you also hold the facts against them over past pain. Not only can you blame and condemn others, or the world, while staying emotionally distant, you also can do that to yourself as well. You can do it with just about anyone or anything. It's an option, a possibility, a choice; just as love, forgiveness and full reconciliation are also options, possibilities, choices. You get to choose, and by choosing, develop spiritually.

# Chapter 19
## With Others

Human beings are social beings, so it is not surprising that we would like to coordinate our efforts at spiritual development with the efforts of others. When acting with others, we can give and receive assistance and we can learn from the experience of others. However, when individuals work together, they often share resources and issues of fairness or equity in the sharing of these resources commonly arise. In the beginning, time may be the only shared resource. And, even if time is the only resource shared by the group, the questions of who is putting in what and who is getting out what can still be important. Some may arrive late or leave early. Some seem to use most of the time for themselves, leaving others with little of the resource. In addition to the main internal obstacles of unfair distribution of costs and benefits and lack of coordination, there are two main external obstacles: lack of autonomy from other groups and lack of coordination with other groups. Fortunately, we know something about the conditions that best facilitate human beings sharing resources for their mutual benefit.

Political scientist Elinor Ostrom received the Nobel prize for economics in 2009 by specifying eight conditions under which groups of individuals can effectively share resources to their mutual benefit by studying groups of individuals who were effectively doing exactly that. These so called, "common-pool resources" included irrigation systems, fisheries, forests, and pastures. Those eight conditions are presented below so that individuals interested in working cooperatively in their spiritual development will have an effective context for doing so.

1. Define clear group boundaries

Clearly defined group boundaries are about who is in and who is out. If several individuals are going to spend time working on their mutual spiritual development, then someone who is present at one meeting and gone for three and back for one and gone for six is not someone who is really in. If time is the resource, they aren't giving theirs in the same way as regularly attending members of the group. The same principle applies regardless of the resource, or resources, in question. This is not being somehow exclusive or exclusionary.

Rather, it is about making clear who is actually a part of the resource-sharing network and who is not. This requirement also underlines that the group is formed for a serious purpose – that all those participating are sufficiently interested and committed to the specified purpose of the group. In this case that purpose is the spiritual development of the group members.

2. Match rules governing use of common goods to local needs and conditions.

Where I come from, one size fit all is the name for the kind of error this second principle aims to avoid. What might work well in one area or location will not necessarily work well everywhere. Consider a group with some members that have young children. What is workable for them is likely to be different than for a group that does not include such individuals. What is workable for individuals that spend much of their time in school may not be workable for individuals who spend much of their time in paid work that may require sticking with more inflexible schedules. Effective rules for one of these groups will likely have been changed in order to be effective for a group composed of both types of individuals. What is workable for individuals with access to a lot of sophisticated technology may not be workable for those who do not and what is workable in a climate with little variation in weather may not be effective in one with wide variation. Rules should vary across conditions because conditions vary.

3. Ensure that those affected by the rules can participate in modifying the rules.

This principle is not only a matter of fairness, equity, or democracy. As a practical matter, when individuals are forced to live with a set of rules about which they have no say, they become more likely to skirt the rules or leave the group. When individuals act this way, the group suffers. This principle helps enhance group cohesiveness and effectiveness.

4. Provide accessible, low-cost means for dispute resolution

Group members are going to disagree. If there is no systematic way to settle these disagreements, then the group will not function well. If the group agrees to start on time, is arriving two minutes late acceptable? How about five, ten, fifteen?

Even when individuals agree to the rules, members may offer different interpretations of those rules. If the established method, or methods, of settling disagreements is cumbersome, complicated, or expensive it will not be regularly used or may not be used at all, and the group will not function well.

Consider flipping a coin as a method of setting a disagreement. It is neither cumbersome, complicated nor expensive, although at least some groups, and some group members, probably will see such a method as too arbitrary. Few folks are likely to agree to regularly settle disagreements based on nothing more than chance even if they might do so occasionally. But the upside of flipping a coin is instructive. It's free and fast. Whatever system of settling disagreements is put in place, the closer it comes to the advantages that come with flipping a coin, namely cheap, easy, and direct, the better it will be. However, the system for settling disagreements also had better address issues like fairness, equity, and mutual respect between group members. Create procedures that address these issues as simply, directly, and cheaply as possible and the group will have effective methods for addressing disagreements.

5. Develop a system, carried out by community members, for monitoring members' behavior.

Unfortunately, people do not always do what they have agreed to do including following the rules of their group. Thus, every group needs a way to determine who is doing their part and who is not. If it is group member A's turn for the group to meet at A's home and everyone arrives to find A is not there, everyone knows, and no special monitoring system is necessary. However, if the group becomes larger and the group activities more complex then lack of follow through may not be so immediately obvious. Group members monitoring member performance highlights who is carrying out the agreed upon arrangements and who is not. No one will have more incentive to ensure that the group runs well than its own members and monitoring the participation of all group members is part of what ensures that the group runs well.

6. Use graduated sanctions for rule violators

If there is no penalty for not following the group rules, then those who fail to follow the rules have little incentive to change. However, it is also important that very high penalties, such as expulsion from the group, not be the first response when individuals fail to do their part. There is a saying: "if there are great penalties for small errors, then there will be no great errors." However, this does not seem to be how it works for groups managing their own resources for their own purposes. Instead, starting with small penalties that grow with continued failure to do one's part has been shown to be more effective. Without monitoring, it is not clear who is doing one's part and who is not. Without penalties, there is no incentive for those for those not doing their part to change. With graduated penalties, there is a proportional response to those not doing their part. While infrequent or occasional rule breaking may still produce some penalties, they are far less severe than frequent or consistent rule breaking for which the penalties become more substantial.

7. Make sure the rule-making rights of community members are respected by outside authorities

If a group of individuals build a social structure to aid one another in their spiritual development and outside forces are able to successfully interfere with group member's ability to participate in that structure, the group simply cannot function properly and perhaps not at all. So, in addition to establishing who is in and who is out of the group, and that all those in the group get their say, the group must also ensure that individuals outside the group cannot interfere with what the group has chosen to do. In part this principle means that if group members know at the beginning, or discover later on, that making certain rules all but guarantees outside interference, then it will be best not to make those rules. If the group cannot achieve functional autonomy in the creation and enforcement of organizational rules that actually work for the group's aim of enhancing the spiritual development of its members, then the group is not going to succeed.

8. Build responsibility for governing the common resource in nested tiers from the lowest level up to the entire interconnected system.

This principle will not be relevant when a few individuals get together to mutually support one another in their pursuit of spiritual development. However, small groups of individuals may grow larger and larger. Groups of individuals may combine with other groups. There is nothing to prevent the development of large, multilayered

103

organizations all of whose members aim at mutually supported spiritual development. As groups of individuals grow in this way, principle 8 becomes more and more important. It emphasizes as much local control as possible at each level and at the same time provides a set of rules that allows compatibility within levels and between levels of the organization. Three separate groups of individuals can use any set of rules that work for them. However, if the three groups are going to cooperate with one another then the rules of each group must be, or become, compatible with the other two. Further if there is a layer of organization above these three groups, the rules at that level must be compatible with the rules used in each of the three lower groups. This principle continues for each additional level above the first.

David Sloan Wilson, a biologist and anthropologist, worked with Elinor Ostrom to situate these principles within evolutionary theory and then, with additional colleagues, to establish both the Prosocial Institute (https:www.prosocial.world/who-we-are) and training for individuals who wish to help groups function more effectively using Ostrom's principles (https://prosocial.teachable.com/courses/prosocial-into-facilitators/lectures/5840079). Those establishing groups to support spiritual development may wish to use these resources.

# Chapter 20
## Willingly ACT:
## Acknowledge, Choose, & Teach Others

"Willingly ACT" provides a practical directive for the principles and practices outlined in this book. Everything begins with willingly acknowledging what is, was or might be. Phrases like "accepting" or "giving my permission" are similar ways of saying the same thing. We can willingly acknowledge what is, was or may be even when we do not approve of it because willing acknowledgement and approval are not the same thing. Few of us are likely to approve of either cancer or injustice. Even so, we can willingly acknowledge both as having occurred in the past, as occurring in the present, and as possibly occurring in the future even as we continue disapproving of the world operating in these ways with which we don't agree. Wisdom asks that we willingly acknowledge even things we do not approve of because arguing with reality doesn't help us deal effectively with it. That remains true whether the reality is experienced inside our skin as thoughts, images, and bodily sensations, or outside our skin as the actions of other living beings or aspects of the non-living universe. Willing acknowledgement is not an alternative to change. It is a prerequisite for our most effective change efforts.

Willingly choosing is the alternative to acting from habit. By waking up to the spiritual aspect of our being, we recognize a place from which we can act with our mind and body but from neither of them. While habits are actions we take quickly and easily and without much awareness, the spiritual aspect of our being provides the capacity to raise our awareness of both what we are doing in any moment of life and what we might do instead. We become aware of what is being made important with our actions and we also become aware of our capacity to willingly choose whether we continue making that important or pick something else. Inside our skin, thoughts and feelings are often pushing us in this way or that, just as we are shoved and enticed by many aspects of the world outside our skin. And even as we willingly acknowledge them from our spiritual center, it is also from our spiritual center that we can willingly choose the directions we travel in life and the ways we travel in those directions, our Leading Principles and values. Together they form a Big Picture of the life we are actually interested in living in contrast to one built solely on habit or at the direction of someone else. From the spiritual aspect of our being, we can then choose to act in the service of that Big Picture regardless of the pushes, shoves or enticements that come from inside and outside our skin. We can even choose to do all this willingly rather than grudgingly. We make contact with the reality that there is nothing we can do that can't be willingly done and then willingly choose which of all those possibilities we will actually perform with our hands, arms, feet, and mouth, right here, right now. With the aspect of our being that remains unchanged by what it notices, we use a Big Picture that is both imminent (right here, right now) and infinite (never used up) to transcend the power of experiences inside or outside our skin to control what we do with our hands, arms, feet, and mouth, in this very moment.

Until now, little has been said about willingly teaching others the principles of spiritual development provided in this book. That, in part, is because you can proceed with your own spiritual development along the lines provided here without ever introducing them to anyone else. That's an option, a possibility. It can be done. However, there are two benefits to willingly pursuing the "T" in ACT.

First, you will find that in trying to make others aware of the approach to spiritual development outlined here, they will misunderstand the approach being offered in ways with which you did not have difficulty. Thus, if you are to succeed in bringing this approach to another, you will be required to widen your own perspective enough to see the world from a perspective that now includes theirs. Engaging this material from that new, wider perspective will deepen your connection to it.

Second, if you sense the approach to spiritual development outlined here might be valuable to other human beings, you will also likely soon recognize that far fewer individuals are likely to make contact with this book than could benefit from the principles and practices contained in it. Your willingness to teach others means they need never contact this book because they have contacted you.

Yes, without bringing these principles and practices to anyone else, you can follow the Formulas for Human Liberation and Serenity in Action. You can awaken to serve the deepest resonances of your being. You can willingly acknowledge, and you can willingly choose. You can willingly do the "A" and the "C." And, since there is nothing you can do that can't be willingly done, you also could choose to willingly add the "T" of teaching others. You can willingly choose to widen the circle of those pursuing this form of spiritual development. You have the choice. You have the option. You could willingly ACT for spiritual development. I hope you will!

Trying to teach an unwilling student is a fool's errand. Alternatively, you might from time to time make efforts to pique someone's interest in the kind of spiritual development offered here. However, until a person shows that interest, you will do better to refrain from attempting to teach these principles no matter how strongly you feel individual might benefit from them. If you spent much time in school, think of all the times you never bothered to learn something or learned it only for a test and then promptly forgot it all the moment the test was over.

One of the best ways to pique interest is to let others see and hear about your efforts to develop spiritually because those efforts are something important to you. Seeing and hearing about something that is important to someone an individual has a connection with can set that individual wondering, "Is that something for me as well?" and create a person who is now interested in what you might have to show them.

Once someone shows an interest, it may often be helpful to use phrases like, "this is how it works for me," "let me show you what someone showed me," or any other phrase that don't make it seem that, "I know and you don't, so you'd better listen up!" Even experts still have something to learn!

What is always available to be learned by anyone engaged in teaching is to view things from the particular perspective of this particular individual learner rather than from the perspective of other learners including your own. It is unlikely that any potential learner will take time to learn any aspect of the spiritual development approach offered here without some sense that their effort will have been worth their time. So, as a teacher, it is important to keep whatever makes the effort worth it to the learner clearly connected to what you, as the teacher, are addressing with that learner. And, whatever that thing is for the learner, it may turn out to be something quite different than it is, or was, for you, the teacher. Said slightly differently, any time a learner asks, "What is the point of learning this?" the answer had better be readily available, with the broadest answer always being, "This will allow me, the learner, to pursue, or better pursue, the life I actually want to live."

Perhaps the most important thing about teaching and learning is that talking about learning isn't learning. Maybe talking about learning can help, but it's not a substitute. Talking about learning to play an instrument is not learning to play an instrument. Learning to play an instrument requires actually attempting to play it. That's where truly effective teaching takes place. An individual is already trying to do something, and they get assistance from someone else in those efforts. Even responses like, "I don't really know how to get started" can be met with, "Here's how." But that only works if the "here's how" is followed by actual starting, rather than talk, or more talk, about starting.

In short, the way to develop spiritually is to make efforts to develop spiritually. When trying to teach, ensure that you are involved with someone actually attempting to develop spiritually rather than only talking about doing so. Why? Because, once again, all the talk in the world about doing something isn't doing it.

If you willingly pursue the "T" in ACT, be ready to willingly admit ignorance, uncertainty, and error. There will be times when a potential learner will ask a question and you won't know how to answer, or you will be in the middle of trying to teach something you realize you don't actually understand or cannot do yourself. Do not try to fake it! If you don't know how to answer a question, then forthrightly admit that you don't know. If you think you might know but are not sure, admit that. Once you have willingly admitted your ignorance or uncertainty, you and the learner can work on how to address that issue.

Perhaps the most difficult thing is willingly admitting error because, "I got that wrong," "I screwed that up." "I sent you down the wrong track" are almost certain to produce feelings of regret in the teacher for having made a mistake about something that was important and annoyance in the learner for the time wasted. Even so, the sooner errors are willingly admitted, the sooner they can be addressed. Error provides opportunities for forgiveness, including self-forgiveness, and reconciliation, two important aspects of spiritual development. The value of readily and willingly admitting ignorance, uncertainty, or error is that you are teaching how these things are best handled. The admissions themselves provide a learning opportunity for you to develop spiritually and for the learner to see that, like her or him, you are just another member of the human family with difficulties and shortcomings of your own. Willingly admitting your ignorance, uncertainty, or error helps your credibility as a person actually trying to help rather than creating the impression you are someone trying to prove they have all the answers for everyone. Indeed, the kind of spiritual development offered here is filled with finding your own way rather than adopting someone else's way.

May this book serve as encouragement and provide effective suggestions for you to willingly teach others and by doing so, more fully, and more fulfillingly, willingly ACT for spiritual development.